A Dog of your own

James Allcock has over thirty years' experience as a vet and is the principal of a mixed practice in Bristol. He is advisor to Bristol Corporation and has been on the council of the British Veterinary Association for the past twelve years. He appears regularly on radio and television programmes including Farming Today, Woman's Hour, and Nationwide. James Allcock lives in Avon (or Somerset as he still prefers to call it), and is married with four children. He is the author of A Cat of Your Own and A Pet Bird of Your Own.

A Dog of your own

James Allcock

Illustrated by Mike Morris

SHELDON PRESS
LONDON

First published in Great Britain in 1979 by
Sheldon Press, Marylebone Road, London NW1 4DU
Third impression (Revised edition) 1987

Printed in Great Britain by
The Camelot Press Ltd, Southampton

ISBN 0 85969 164 0

Contents

Acknowledgements

To veterinary surgeons Mike Stockman and Neal King whose comments on the manuscript added greatly to the finished text. To 'maid of all work' Jenny Botsford, literary agent, guide and typist, who introduced punctuation into this book and introduced me to punctuation.

and
Dedicated to
Cradbury Flash Beauty—Kennel name Georgina—a Staffordshire bull terrier bitch so unfeminine she's called GEORGE.

Foreword

Jim Allcock is at one and the same time a scientist with a balanced view of his job and an entertainer of no small merit. Ask him a question and no matter how complex or abstruse it may be, it will receive a straightforward answer. No one person has done more to put the veterinary viewpoint to the ordinary man or woman and in this book Jim performs the very difficult task of preaching to the unconverted without seeming to be laying down the law.

It has become very obvious over the past few years that the place of the dog in modern society is no longer sacred and guaranteed. People actually dare to criticize dogs in the paper and on radio and television; such action would once have brought angry dog-lovers striding into editorial offices brandishing horse-whips!

As a reaction the veterinary profession has taken upon itself the role of teacher, and has proclaimed the doctrine of 'Responsible Petmanship'. If that suggests that Jim Allcock's book is therefore likely to be a pompous diatribe full of condescending instructions, nothing could be further from the truth. The message comes over loud and clear: Think hard before you take on a dog at all; think again about what sort and size of dog is right for you and yours; and once you have acquired the newcomer to the household, teach it to behave in such a fashion that it will never be a nuisance to other people while the two of you, owner and pet, derive all the pleasure there is in a very special relationship.

Whether you are contemplating purchasing your first dog, or are a seasoned owner who is asked for help by novices, this book will give you help in an amusing down-to-earth way. You may have heard the message before, but never in so readable a style.

Michael Stockman
President, British Veterinary Association

A Dog of your own

Shall we?

'Till death us do part' is not only a phrase from the marriage service and the title of a television series, it's also the thought that should be in your mind when you first start thinking of buying a puppy. There is a strong likelihood that the puppy you're about to buy will be part of your family for the next fourteen years or so. Choose wisely, slowly, and sensibly.

First—should you have a dog at all? It's almost easier to define those situations where you should choose a cat, budgie or goldfish instead. If you're single, switched on, live in a bed sitter and only come home to sleep then you're not for a dog. Even a goldfish might get lonely. If you're married flat dwellers, both out at work and constantly away at weekends, the same applies.

But if you're in a house or flat with some sort of outside space available and not too house proud, if you and your family like animals, then a dog is the pet which best fits into the family. He's more a part of the family than a cat, he can come out with you and the children, he can even join the family holiday.

If the answer to 'Shall we?' is 'Yes' the next question is:

What sort?

There are two ways of asking this question (*a*) What sort of owner are you? and (*b*) What sort of dog should you have?

Are you energetic enough to exercise a big, active dog, energetic enough to groom a long-haired dog regularly? Is your house—and fireside—big enough for a really large dog, will he fit in the car?

It is also very useful to have a dog that is small enough to pick u

Are you house proud, will you worry about a few dog hairs and the pitter patter of muddy feet? Are you tough enough to control one of the more aggressive breeds?

If you are a five foot nothing, frail female, living in a tiny cottage with an elderly mother and drive a bubble car don't choose a Great Dane. If you are an enthusiastic hill walker and have visions of romping the open country followed by your faithful hound then don't choose a Chihuahua or a Miniature Yorkshire Terrier.

Many dog owners are slightly lazy—and there is nothing wrong with that—so unless you really want to make work for yourself choose an 'easy' dog. Short hairs mean much less combing. Hairless feet mean much less mud in the house. A dog that doesn't need clipping or stripping means that you don't have to arrange extra hair appointments and take him to them.

It's also very useful to have a dog that is small enough to pick up. If you've got to travel by bus it's upstairs for both of you and while you might train the big dog to walk upstairs you'll easily carry the little one.

No doubt the canines in France exclaim '*Vive la différence*' and there is a 'difference' in dogs—which leads to:

What sex?

You must decide—don't just pick what's left.

Pros and cons. Bitches tend to be gentler, their maternal instincts often make them kinder with children. They are cleaner around the garden—don't cock their legs on the cabbages. Heat is a nuisance but it only happens for three weeks twice a year. Unwanted puppies can be an embarrassment but these happen only if the owner is unwatchful.

Dogs tend to be more aggressive, there is no heat trouble of course but they tend to wander to visit their girl friends.

In both sexes neutering is possible. This operation is known as spaying in the bitch and, of course, castration in the dog. The purpose is to render the animal neuter not merely to stop him or her procreating, so tying the tubes in the bitch or vasectomy in the dog are quite impractical in that all the nuisance of a fully sexed animal remains, only results are prevented. The section on neutering deals with this question in greater detail.

How much?

Unless you are a multi-millionaire or Government it is as well to see if you can afford to indulge your pleasures.

What's a dog budget likely to be?

Cost of dog.   Cross bred Free–£30
                             Pedigree £60–£200

Top class show dogs can cost much more, but unless you are keen on competitive showing it is gross extravagance to pay the show prices.

Basket or box, say £5–£40
Collar and lead £4–£12
Feeding/Water bowl £3

Do let the dog have his own. It's not good hygiene to interchange his and yours and you don't want the children claiming it's their turn to eat off Toby's plate.

Running costs. Once you've spent between £12 and £150 in 'capital expenditure' you've committed yourself to a weekly extra on your household budget.

Feeding is the main item. How, what and how much comes later but in very round figures any dog will cost nearly £2.50 per week to feed and the larger breeds three times as much. You can make feeding expensive and it is surprising how many owners take a pride in the high cost of feeding their dog, but there's no need to.

Veterinary fees are modest compared with the basic feeding costs. Obviously there is a great variation depending on the luck of the dog (and the care of the owner).

Distemper/hard pad/hepatitis/leptospira and parvovirus vaccination is essential, the cost is £15–£22 in the first year and thereafter an annual booster will cost about £10.

Many dogs, most dogs, go from year to year without any need for treatment until they reach the inevitable old age troubles. But of course accidents happen, paws get cut, infections get caught.

It is probable that the average dog does not need £150 worth of veterinary attention in his life, but it may be that in one year his veterinary account could be as much, or more than this. There are insurances to cover veterinary fees. Premiums vary—and so do the 'small print clauses'—but about £25 per year will often cover all veterinary fees after the first £10. Less than the washing machine or TV costs to insure.

A **Licence** is still required although there are suggestions that the Government will abolish it or transfer licensing functions to District Councils. At present a licence costs 37p. It may cost £5 or nothing in the future, but either way it is a minor item in a dog budget.

Holidays for you might mean kennels for your dog. A fortnight will cost between £30 and £45. If you kennel your bitch when she is on heat this will mean three weeks, twice a year and so cost £50–£80 per year. (There is a pill or injection to postpone or shorten heat, depending on the size of the bitch; this will cost £3–£7·50 per heat.)

So in one paragraph ...

	Low Estimate £	High Estimate £
Unavoidable costs		
Feeding	125.00	350.00
Holidays	Nil	45.00
Veterinary (Booster only)	10.00	100.00
Licence	0.37	5.00
	135.37	500.00
Possible costs		
First year		
Vaccination	15.00	25.00
Neutering	Nil	60.00
Childhood troubles	Nil	50.00
Season, kennels	Nil	100.00
Overall total	£ 150.37	735.00

Thus a minimum budget is about £3 per week for a small dog and bigger ones needing clipping, stripping and kennelling can cost more than £15 per week.

How? Where?

If you've got this far and decided 'Yes' how do you go about buying your dog? Slowly is the first answer, and don'ts are as long a list as do's.

DON'T buy the last miserable puppy in a pet shop window because you are sorry for him.

DON'T buy any puppy that seems less than healthy, slightly lame, or has any obvious blemishes.

DON'T take notice of bland assurances by the seller that 'all puppies have fleas/diarrhoea/funny lumps/three legs' or what have you. They don't.

DO buy from the breeder of the puppy—and see mother. There are two very important reasons for this. First, it is a considerable stress to any young animal to change homes. An eight-week-old puppy can cope with this given reasonable care. However, he finds it difficult going first to a kennels or pet shop, mixing with older pups from other sources, changing food, and then as soon as he is accustomed to this, changing again to your home, your routine and your feeding.

Secondly, seeing mum is important because it gives you some clue as to the possible temperament of the puppy. If she is highly nervous or very aggressive it is probable that her offspring will have the same unfortunate tendencies. If you can see father as well this is even better.

Wasn't it Oscar Wilde who said, 'All women grow like their mothers'? So if you're attracted to mother then you've probably found the puppy you want.

DO refuse a puppy that is not what you are looking for. If you have decided to have a bitch and the only ones left are dogs, wait or look

If you're attracted to mother, you've probably found the puppy you want

elsewhere. Even if it is Lindy Lou's birthday don't make the birthday a happy event and spend the next ten years or more wishing you hadn't.

DO   buy a puppy you've seen. There is a strong inexplicable feeling amongst some potential purchasers that anything bought from a long way away must be better. Thus some poor puppy is bought by someone living in Cornwall from a home in Scotland and at the same time an Aberdonian is awaiting the arrival of a puppy from Cornwall. These puppies travel by rail, unaccompanied. Almost every railwayman is good with all livestock and every veterinary surgeon has experience of the care and trouble that porters take with livestock but with the best care in the world a twelve-hour journey, which may be too hot, may be too cold, certainly hungry, thirsty and confused is not a good or pleasant start in life for any puppy. If the only puppy you can find is a long way off then go and collect him yourself.

How many?

So far we've talked about a puppy—definitely singular. There is often a very good case for having two puppies. They are company for each other. If you have to leave your dog at home for several hours each day you can do it with a much clearer conscience if he has got company. Two puppies are often less destructive than one. Boredom is often the cause of your puppy eating the furniture. No matter how many toys you give him the toys don't play with him. However, if there are two puppies they can chew each other, instead of the furniture.

House training might be more difficult with two—each is inclined to copy the other's mistakes, and it is essential to train two puppies 'in tandem'.

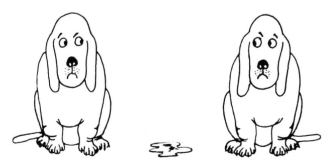

House training may be more difficult with two . . .

Breeds

There are more than 150 breeds of dogs recognized by the Kennel Club—the governing body of the U.K. dog world—and there are an infinite number of mixtures of the recognized breeds.

Let's get a few terms clear:

Pure bred means mother and father were of the same breed.
Cross bred means mother and father were of different breeds. They may each be a pure bred, in which case

Pedigree

Cross bred

Mongrel

the puppy is a *first cross*. If a labrador bitch met a pointer dog, the resulting puppies would be cross breds and could be called first cross pointers or first cross labradors. They would probably look alike, and behave like a mixture of the two breeds. If the same bitch went astray with an already cross bred dog, the resulting puppies would be well described as *mongrels*, and their size and behaviour would be less easy to predict.

A *Pedigree* dog is a pure bred one, whose ancestors are known and the pedigree is the piece of paper that lists the ancestors. A pedigree is written by the breeder of the puppy and this pedigree may be registered at the Kennel Club on payment of a fee.

A pedigree is shown on the following page.

The parents of the puppy have each 50 per cent influence on it, the grandparents 25 per cent each, the great-grandparents $12\frac{1}{2}$ per cent each or one eighth, and the great-great-grandparents one sixteenth. So don't take too much notice of very distant ancestors and even less notice if it was the brother of the great-great-grandmother who won a championship. This relationship is just too distant to be of any importance. If your grandmother's great-uncle's cousin was hanged for sheep-stealing, it doesn't mean that a leg of New Zealand lamb is in danger every time you enter the supermarket!

How does all this affect you if you are going to buy a puppy?

If you buy a pure bred puppy you'll have a very good idea of what size, shape, colour and even temperament he's going to grow up to be. If he's got a pedigree as well, you *might*, if the pedigree has some show-winning ancestors freely distributed through the generations, have a puppy that will do well in the show-ring.

BREED **XY HOUND**

SEX **DOG**

COLOUR and MARKINGS **BLACK**

DATE OF BIRTH **13.6.78**

KENNEL NAME

"OUR DOGS"
PEDIGREE FORM

Kennel Club Club Registration Certificate No. **7841/86**

Date of Registration **20.6.78**

Kennel Club Stud Book No.

BRED BY **A. Breeder, Canineton**

OWNED BY **J. Brown, 78 Church St Dogsville**

Pedigree of WOTSIT JASON

PARENTS	GRAND PARENTS	G.G. PARENTS	G.G.G. PARENTS (2)
SIRE GLENTY LIVELY (1) 9973/132	**SIRE** GLENTY TOM	**SIRE** WOTSIT SAM	**SIRE** TOPLESS TOT
			DAM WOTSIT AGATHA
		DAM GLENTY JOAN	**SIRE** CH.(3) RHUBARB MIKE
			DAM GLENTY ANN
	DAM GLENTY MYRTLE	**SIRE** WOTSIT SAM	**SIRE** CH. REDSTONE RANDY
			DAM CH. WOTSIT GIRL
		DAM CH. BITING BERTHA	**SIRE** CH. TENTREES TOM
			DAM BITING JANET
DAM WOTSIT JANET 1234/74 (4)	**SIRE** CH. RHUBARB JOE	**SIRE** RHUBARB SAM	**SIRE** CH. RHUBARB MIKE
			DAM RHUBARB PINK EYE
		DAM RHUBARB RED PET	**SIRE** CH. REDSTONE RANDY
			DAM RHUBARB ACACIA
	DAM WOTSIT KATE	**SIRE** RHUBARB MIKE	**SIRE** POTTERY PETER
			DAM RHUBARB MIMOSA
		DAM WOTSIT JANE	**SIRE** WOTSIT SAM
			DAM WOTSIT RED ROSE

SIGNED **A Breeder** DATE **10.8.78**

Published by 'Our Dogs' Publishing Co. Ltd. Oxford Road Station Approach. Manchester. 1. (Copyright).

(1) Glenty = Registered prefix   (2) A champion in the great-great-grandparent generation has little influence on the actual puppy four generations later   (3) CH = Champion, usually written in red   (4) 74 = Kennel Club registration number

There's another advantage of pedigrees in some breeds. There are inherited faults and defects in any species of animal and sometimes these defects can appear by breeding together closely related animals. These defects are well recognized and the Kennel Club and the British Veterinary Association have organized two certification schemes whereby the parents are examined for freedom from these inherited diseases. If you buy a puppy from parents certified free from these diseases there is a fair chance that whatever else troubles your puppy, it won't be one of these inherited defects.

The major inherited faults are:

Hip dysplasia

This is commoner in the larger breeds, and is a defect of the hip joint whereby the socket of the ball-and-socket joint that forms the hip is much too shallow. As a result the ball part of the joint doesn't fit snugly—in extreme cases doesn't fit at all—just slips out giving an actual dislocated hip. But even if it's not bad enough to dislocate, the movement of the ball within the wrong shaped socket leads to arthritis of the joint and lameness.

The degree of trouble caused by hip dysplasia varies enormously from complete disabling dislocation to merely a slight lameness late in life.

An X-ray is taken of the hips after the dog has been anaesthetized and carefully positioned to show the shape of the hip joint. This can tell us just how good is the shape of the ball and socket.

The pictures are examined by a panel of veterinary surgeons who are very experienced in reading X-rays. On the basis of their report the dog may be certified as free of any sign of hip dysplasia.

Thus, if your puppy is from two parents, each certified under the BVA/Kennel Club Hip Dysplasia

Control Scheme, there is a better chance that puppy's hips will be free of trouble also.

Progressive retinal atrophy and hereditary cataract

The BVA/Kennel Club/International SheepDog Society Eye Scheme is intended to ensure that breeding stock are free from any inheritable abnormalities of the eye. These include PRA which is a degeneration of the retina (the area at the back of the eyeball that collects the image before it is passed on to the brain). Affected dogs may become blind at any time between two and six years of age. Hereditary cataract makes the lens opaque so light cannot reach the retina. There is an inherited trouble in Collie breeds known as Collie Eye Anomaly which can sometimes be detected as early as eight weeks of age and so puppy examination can be of value in some cases.

Examination of the eye, using an ophthalmoscope which allows one to examine the inside of the eye, establish normality and if a breeding dog or bitch is examined and found normal—again by one of an appointed panel of examiners—he or she can be registered as free from inheritable eye disorders.

There are a number of other inherited troubles which are not the subject of control schemes. Slipping patella (knee-caps) in small breeds, entropion (in-turning of eyelashes in chows and some spaniels), districhiasis (a double row of eyelashes in pekes) and excessive nervousness or aggressiveness can be major inherited defects.

Don't get too worried. There are bad apples in any box but they're few.

When you're buying, ask questions. Think about these control schemes, and best of all have your puppy 'vetted' before purchase. Any veterinary surgeon will be willing to see a puppy before you buy it, and advise. The vet knows the sort of troubles to expect and can warn you if any are present. Some breeders resent such an examination of their stock; they seem to feel it is casting doubt on their morals or morality. Stuff and nonsense. This sort of examination has been the rule in the horse trade for generations. Where else did the verb 'to vet' originate? Cost of such an examination is £7–£12 at the veterinary surgery, more of course if travelling is involved.

Inoculations

Every puppy should be vaccinated before he begins to go out and mix with other dogs or goes out where other dogs have been.

The diseases that he can be protected against are:

Distemper and hard pad
Infectious hepatitis
Leptospirosis
Canine parvovirus

Lots of long names. What are they?

Distemper, which includes hard pad, is a disease caused by a virus which affects dogs of all ages and kills almost half of those that catch the disease.

Young animals of 4–8 months are most frequently affected, not because they're young but simply because they catch the disease from other dogs as soon as they're old enough to go out and meet infection.

The first signs are very vague; an unwell dog, a bit of a cough, half-closed eyes, especially in bright light, slightly off food, and maybe a bit of diarrhoea. Then he seems to get a bit better, then worse, then better. After about ten days, there is often a yellow discharge from the eyes and nose.

Very often the owner finds lots of explanations for the illness. Worms, mother gone on holiday, next door's dog chased him, but finally it dawns. The dog is ill, very ill.

The dangerous part of distemper is towards the end of the disease, as much as six or eight weeks after the first signs. This is when the virus can get into the nervous system and the brain where it can cause uncontrollable fits or a paralysis of one or more legs or an uncontrollable twitch; St Vitus's dance.

The nervous damage is almost always incurable and leads to the death of the dog or destruction because continued life is quite unreasonable. A horrid, heartbreaking disease.

Infectious hepatitis is another virus infection less common than distemper but in its acute form can kill a dog in twenty-four hours.

Leptospirosis is a bacterial infection. There are two sorts; Canicola, so called 'lamp post disease', which damages the kidneys of dogs and is spread in the urine of infected animals. This damage, often occurring in the first year or so of life can lead to kidney trouble in middle age. The other form, rarer, is the same infection as Weil's disease in the human. This is the jaundice type disease spread by rats. It is not very common in dogs but is a potential killer.

Parvovirus

In 1978 a new disease of dogs appeared called parvovirus. There's nothing magic about the name, it just means 'little virus'. The first signs that something new was about were unexplained deaths of apparently healthy, 6–10-weeks-old puppies from heart failure in kennels where older dogs had suffered attacks of sickness and diarrhorea, sometimes mild attacks, sometimes very severe ones.

Vets at the Glasgow Veterinary School identified and isolated the cause. Veterinary detective work discovered the offender very quickly and ample evidence was uncovered to incriminate this new virus. Although it is new, parvovirus is closely related to the long known virus which causes feline infectious enteritis. There is no direct connection. Dogs do not catch parvovirus from cats but this relationship meant that cat enteritis vaccine could be used to protect dogs from parvovirus.

In the dog, parvovirus chooses rapidly dividing cells in which to live. Very young puppies, less than 4 weeks of age, have rapidly growing hearts and heart muscle cells, so the virus will damage the heart *in very young puppies*. As the dog grows older the heart cells are no longer rapidly dividing, but those cells lining the stomach and intestine are always dividing and being renewed. So in the older puppy and the adult dog the virus grows in these intestinal cells—hence the symptoms of vomiting and diarrhoea. An extreme depression is also most obvious but you, as an owner, should not be too concerned about symptoms. Your job as a good owner is to recognize that the dog is not well. Your vet is the person to diagnose the cause of any illness.

Parvovirus has now established itself as one of the hazards of life as a dog, but there are now a number of vaccines made especially for use in dogs which give very good protection. Because so many breeding bitches are immune, and pass some of this immunity to their puppies while they are suckling, the heart damage resulting from parvovirus is much less common than it was in the early days of the disease.

The impact of parvovirus varies in different parts of the country so at any time the best and most up-to-date advice about your dog in your area will come from your vet. Ask him.

These are the diseases which inoculation of puppies is intended to prevent.

No vaccination in humans or animals will ever be 100 per cent perfect. You will hear of this dog and that dog being vaccinated and still getting the disease. Maybe the story you hear is true, but modern vaccines are good, very good indeed, and a near perfect protection against all these unpleasant diseases can be obtained.

When is the time to vaccinate? In specific terms ask your vet. He knows the local disease situation, but in

general terms as soon as possible once the puppy has
settled down into his new home. You may be told by a
breeder or seller of a puppy 'get him inoculated
right away', you telephone your vet and he says 'wait
a fortnight'. Already you're confused, who do you
believe?

Believe your vet. Here's the logic behind it.

The inoculations do not give your puppy protection, they make him create his own immunity. This is
a basic principle of immunity in animals or man.
Either we can give a dog immunity, and having given
him the antibodies against the disease he gets immediate protection which soon wears out, or we can give
him something to make him make antibodies and
make his immunity. There's a time-lag while he makes
his immunity, but because its a homemade immunity
it lasts much longer than a merely borrowed one. The
young puppy who has just changed homes is busy
coping with a change of home, surroundings, diet,
meeting new germs, and all these stresses and strains
mean that he's not going to make a very good
immunity if he's inoculated at the same time as he
changes home. No harm is done by inoculating at this
time, but it may be that not enough good is done.
There can be some residual immunity that the puppy
has obtained via mother's milk and this can prevent
good protection. The normal procedure is two injections at an interval of two to four weeks. There are a
number of different makes of the vaccines and the
precise procedure varies a little, so ask your vet.

One possible pitfall in this inoculation question.
Human measles vaccine will give a fairly good protection against distemper for a few months. Some
kennels use this vaccine on six-week-old puppies and
may tell you that the puppy has been inoculated
against distemper. So it has, but not a very long-
lasting protection. If you buy a puppy that has been

inoculated get a certificate of inoculation—if you don't quite understand the certificate your vet will, and he'll be able to tell you if it's a complete protection or merely a short term one.

Booster vaccination

Any immunity wears out, and so it needs 'boosting' now and again. We see this in human disease in such a simple thing as a 'flu epidemic. One year, there is a lot of real influenza and every third person seems to get it. Then a few years pass with very little until a new epidemic occurs. What happens is that the human population acquires an immunity after the first epidemic and then three or four years later when the immunity has worn out, another epidemic is possible.

Dogs can get boosters by natural infection from the nearest lamp post and so enhance their immunity. But one doesn't know if they have, and so artificial boosters are wise.

Lord Thomson once said that half of all advertising is wasted, but would someone please tell him which half. Similar are boosters. Many dogs keep their immunity topped up by meeting germs from their low friends and some boosters are wasted in that they are not needed. But for safety, peace of mind and your dog's sake, it's worth having a booster injection every one or two years just to make sure.

There's an apparent paradox here. The dog who leads the most protected and secluded life needs boosters most. His immunity has least stimulation from natural germs and can almost disappear. Then if he should meet infection, he and you are in trouble.

Again with boosters, consult your vet. He knows the local disease situation best. The whole subject of vaccination is more than just sticking needles in dogs.

It's using the right vaccine at the right time for your dog to get the right and best effect.

Neutering

Over-population is in vogue, or rather concern about it is. This applies to dogs as well as humans. Neutering of male or female dogs is in some part an attempt to prevent the birth of unwanted puppies but mainly one should consider neutering in the context of making the dog or bitch a more acceptable animal in his or her human environment. 'It's not natural' is the immediate reaction. Neither is keeping dogs in houses or eating meat from castrated bulls, boars or rams. The 'natural' dog in this context ceased to exist in this country centuries ago. There are wild dogs in parts of the world. They live in packs, full of fleas, with unkempt coats, as savage hunting animals. We, the human race, have selected dogs, bred them to have 'unnatural' characteristics and we keep them in houses, and very much pleasanter characters and companions they have turned out to be.

We have not removed natural sexual instincts from the dog, but we do restrict his sexual behaviour. Sometimes the result is a frustrated and unhappy dog. Social nuisances result. The bitch on heat encourages dogs to collect around her house, the silence of the small hours is disturbed, not to mention the neighbour's garden!

The wandering dog can, and does, cause traffic accidents in his journeys to and from his lady loves. The confined dog, especially the smaller breeds, has a tendency to do embarrassing things with cushions, which act as a conversation stopper rather than adding to the joys of dog owning.

'Moral' reasons against neutering either sex are not really tenable. What about practical considerations? In the dog the operation is castration, the surgical removal of the testicles. One is concerned with

He can cause traffic accidents in his journeys to and from his lady loves

rendering the dog neuter, not merely preventing him fathering puppies and so vasectomy, as in the human, does not fulfil the purpose desired. The hormones which make the dog act as a male, are the hormones which are produced in the testicles, which must be removed. Apart from making the dog non-sexual, castration does reduce male aggressiveness.

In the bitch the operation is spaying, or to be scientific, ovaro-hysterectomy. The ovaries and the uterus are removed by a surgical operation. The bitch does not come on heat, and so as well as not producing puppies, all the nuisance from hopeful dogs is avoided. Both operations must, of course, be performed under a general anaesthetic. This usually involves your pet in a day or a day and night away from home. By the morning after, he or she should be feeling and behaving as though there hadn't been a night before!

Neutering does have effects, if there were no effects there would be no reason for neutering, *but* the effects are not *ill*-effects. If a neutered dog is overfed, it will get fat, but this obesity is the result of too much food, not an operation. Almost all guide dogs for the blind are neutered. No one is going to trust a blind person's life to a less than properly functioning dog, and one sees very few over-fat guide dogs.

The final decision is and must be yours. There are advantages in neutering and there may be more queries than I have answered here. Telephone your vet, go and see your vet. He'll advise you.

Feeding

Feeding dogs seems to cause more heart-searching and guilt complexes among owners than any other aspect of dog keeping.

Obviously feeding is a fundamental, maybe the fundamental, part of owning a dog but it is possible to make it fairly simple.

It is convenient to talk about feeding dogs as one aspect and feeding a puppy as another. In this context a fair definition of the puppy is a young animal up to say 10 months old. Why 10 months? Let's consider a few landmarks in a puppy's development.

0–3 weeks—mother's milk only.

6–8 weeks, and the puppy is weaning. Solid food may start at 3 weeks and by 8 weeks old mother's milk has finished.

$3\frac{1}{2}$ months—the first temporary (baby or milk) teeth are shed and permanent teeth replace them.

6 months or just after—all the permanent teeth are there.

10–12 months, and growth has almost ceased.

He may grow heavier and fatter but not taller or longer. The smaller breeds are sexually mature and can even have achieved parenthood. The average puppy is about 100 times heavier when he's a year old than he was at birth. A human baby is said to increase four times in weight in the first year of life. Large breed puppies may gain 4 ounces *per day*. If a human baby of this age made such a weight gain in a week you would write to tell Granny all about it.

In a puppy everything happens quickly and the feeding requirements change quite a lot during the first year of life. After 10 months–1 year old the dog has only to stay alive and find energy—the extra food for growing at a considerable pace is not needed, and if it is supplied it is simply converted to fat.

Food provides for energy, for growth, for renewal and repair of the body, but it also provides occupation and the satisfaction of a full stomach. Eating hard food or large pieces of food means that the teeth are used and cleaned.

All the preceding section might read like the political speeches that are the rule nowadays when a number of irrefutable facts are joined together and the speaker hopes that these statements will be accepted as a substitute for positive policies. Maybe it is accepted by the humans who are vote fodder but your dog has more basic ideas. He wants food now, and tomorrow. He wants action.

Let's divide practical feeding in four ways.

What sort?
How much?
How often?
What size?

What sort?

Dogs thrive on the most extraordinary varieties of foods. All vets are asked how to feed dogs. No vet can look at a dog and say 'Ah, there's a red meat fed dog' or 'There's a *Bla Bla's Complete Dog Food* fed dog'. In fact the dog is very adaptable.

In general terms again, the dog is a meat eating animal and he needs some animal protein in one form or another. He can live very well on meat alone, getting his protein, carbohydrate, fat, minerals and vitamins from meat. You'll probably be much poorer and your dog might well have some trouble with diarrhoea. A compromise—totally acceptable to the dog and much easier on your pocket—is some meat and biscuits, brown bread, surplus family food to make up.

Meat

Whether the meat is supplied as raw meat, cooked meat or from tinned foods is quite immaterial. Decide which is more convenient and economical for you. Which make of tinned food is again up to you. The major pet food manufacturers are highly reputable and there is no doubt that the foods they produce are quite suitable and adequate for any dog. The quality varies in that some foods have more meat than others—some are designed to be fed alone and are cheaper per tin, some are designed to be fed with biscuits or scraps and are dearer per tin. In every case the tin tells you—so read the instructions, remembering these are not a canine version of the Ten Commandments. They are a good, reliable guide to the feeding values of a particular make of food if you forget the advertising agent's superlatives.

Fish can be used on occasions in place of the meat. One might hesitate to recommend a diet entirely of fish, but as a twice weekly alternative it is quite satisfactory.

Biscuits

Biscuits, like manufactured tinned foods, come in all shapes, varieties and sizes and are all pretty satisfactory. Some contain much more meat meal than others, some are intended as complete feeds.

Household scraps

These can properly be used to feed your dog and help your pocket. Use common sense at the same time. Sense as to quantity, 'richness' and constituents.

A very common bit of dog lore is that dogs must not eat potatoes. A certain number of dog owners appear to believe that their dog will collapse and die should he take a mouthful of potato. Nonsense! Of course large quantities of potatoes regularly will lead to a very fat dog, but if he has the odd potato, the odd chip, he is not going to come to any harm. If you eat seven pounds of strawberries tonight you'll be awfully ill—this doesn't mean that strawberries are wrong.

The real danger with household scraps is obesity (of the dog). Left-over crusts, bits of pie, regular potatoes, surplus roast beef fat, baby's custard and unfinished rusk are all highly fattening foods—as well as being very tasty to the dog.

How much?

One of the very difficult questions to answer. You have to learn this by finding out what *your* dog thrives upon. If your dog is overweight there is a one word answer to How much? ... Less.

As a general guide $\frac{1}{4}-\frac{1}{2}$ oz of food per day per pound of weight of the dog is about normal. The smaller dog eats proportionately more food than the large one. These are suggestions for the adult dog. Puppies, of course, will eat much more. It is difficult to over-feed a puppy under six months old and the best method of deciding how much to give to a puppy is to leave it to the puppy. Make each feed as much as he will eat in 15 minutes.

How often?

Puppies need to be fed more often than the adult dog.

As a working suggestion:

2–3 months old	4 meals per day
3–5 months old	3 meals per day
5–9 months old	2 meals per day
Adult dogs	1 meal per day

These frequencies are a reasonable guide but you will not burn in the eternal fires of hell if you feed

4 meals on the day your puppy is 3 months and 1 day old.

The largest meal should be the last one at night. Most animals eat and sleep and a full tummy is one of the best soporifics. Just think how you feel after a heavy lunch.

In very hot weather you'll find that many dogs prefer to feed in the cool of the evening and a 10-o'clock feed is eaten with more relish than one offered at 6 p.m. and 90°F air temperature.

You may find that your puppy decides his own feeding routine by being less enthusiastic about a morning feed as he grows up. He knows best and if this is so, stop that particular meal time.

Feeding late in the evening will not make your dog dirty at night. On the contrary. Food takes at least 12 hours to travel from stem to stern—or mouth to anus—and a midday feed is more likely to be ready to be evacuated through the night than an evening one. In any case, normal training means that the dog's own intestinal clock works as you would wish.

What size?

Not how much is in the dish but how big are the pieces of meat, biscuit or what have you. Dogs have teeth, an obvious remark, but some dog owners don't seem to realize that the teeth are there to be used on food. As you will have seen on p. 23, by 6–8 months a dog has all the teeth that he's ever going to have.

Dogs don't 'chew' food the way that we do. They use their teeth to tear food into conveniently sized pieces—and a conveniently sized piece appears by human standards to be a very large one. The average sized terrier will swallow a golf ball, or a large sausage whole and in the case of the sausage, digest it quite successfully.

There is no need to cut food into near-pinhead sized pieces even for the smallest dog. He can do the cutting—he's got more time to spare than you have. Some owners appear to think that part of their duty is to slice, even mince meat for their dog, and at the same time show the latest wounds that the little dear's teeth have inflicted on their hand. Why the dog who can drive his teeth deep into the hand that feeds him cannot be expected to drive them into a piece of meat is beyond comprehension and—just to digress a moment—*raw meat does not* make a dog fierce.

There are certain advantages in giving large pieces—or one large piece of food to your dog. You save time, he takes time, and feeding is a very pleasant way of passing time. If the day's feeding is finished in two minutes flat a very useful period of occupation has been let pass.

Large pieces make the dog eat more slowly and in his tearing of food, saliva is mixed with the food. These two factors alone must help digestion.

The greatest benefit of large pieces of food is to the teeth themselves. Unused teeth are uncleaned teeth and tartar accumulates on them. This tartar pushes the gums away from the roots of the teeth, the tooth sockets become infected and the gums soft and unhealthy—pyorrhoea in fact. There is a considerable amount of tooth trouble in dogs—not toothache which in the human is often actual decay in the tooth—but infection of the gums and tooth sockets. Hard work by the teeth, driving them into a piece of tough meat or cracking biscuits, will clean them and prevent accumulation of tartar. The dog who works for his living with his teeth tends to die of old age with nice white teeth. It's the 'well cared for, Welfare State' dog which never uses his teeth on food at all that needs dental attention at four, five, six years old and reaches old age with two teeth only in his head.

All this leads us to bones which are not a food for any dog. They may be a useful toothbrush, entertainment, but not food. Of course the wild dog ate bones but he did not eat undiluted bone. He caught a rabbit, or more likely found a rabbit that had died of old age, and ate a bit of flesh, bit of fur, bit of bone, bit of liver, all mixed up together. When we give a dog a bone it's often cooked, all the fat, meat and general 'goo' boiled out of it. In fact, it's rather like concrete. The dog grinds up this mineral mixture and eats it, the pieces of bone reset, rather like concrete, in the rectum. The result may be a very constipated dog.

Two other troubles that can result from bones: vomiting if the bone bits irritate the stomach. Messy but not serious. But it could happen that a bone sticks in the oesophagus and this *is* very serious. It's often a chop bone or the end of a lamb bone. Just too big to swallow. Often it's a bone the dog has stolen and in his efforts to hide it quickly he swallows it. The bone can get as far as the middle of the oesophagus on its way to the stomach. Then it gets stuck. Nasty, difficult to remove and a fairly major operation at the best. Of course lots of dogs have lots of bones and no harm results. Vets only see the troubles. If you want to be very safe only give your dog such an impossibly big and hard bone that he cannot swallow it or break it up. As soon as the bone starts to disintegrate, take it away.

Most of the advantages of bone can be obtained by giving a really large biscuit as the toothbrush/ plaything. If a piece of biscuit gets stuck it will dissolve. Bone will not.

Julius Caesar wanted *men* about him that were fat— or so we are told. Even in those days he did not want obese dogs. Obesity is as big a problem in the modern dog as the modern human. There are not the same

risks of coronary heart disease in the dog but there's
no doubt that the overweight dog has a poorer
quality of life, particularly in older age. Any arthritis
resulting from wear and tear of the years is much
more painful in the overweight animal. The effort required to carry around many excess pounds just isn't
there in the old dog and he drifts into a stagnant
limbo, with food his only interest, little pleasure to
himself and none to his owner.

Weight does not just appear overnight. It's an in-
sidious process of storing excess food for a rainy day.
Rather like the camel with his hump. If the rainy day
doesn't appear weight gain continues.

A spaniel that should weigh about 26 lb need only
gain 2 oz per month to be nearly 10 lb overweight by
the time he's seven. Then you decide to slim your dog
and to take off the weight of seven years in three
months. Poor dog, his world has come to an end.
Much better to stop this happening. Don't let the
excess weight build up.

Yes, it's difficult, when you see your dog every day,
to notice the first signs of overweight. Scales help.
Weigh him at a year old, then every six months.
You'll soon see if a steady increase is occurring in time
to check it after the first two or three pounds.

Use your bathroom scales for weighing yourself,
then you holding the dog. A slight calculation gives
you the dog's weight. Sorry to point this out but
often an owner finds it impossible to weigh the dog
because the dog will not sit still on the scales.

The answer to excess weight is less food; there is no
other answer. Exercise helps a little but food quantity
is critical. So often exercise merely makes the dog feel
fitter and hungrier so that, owner permitting, he eats
more as a result.

All feeding is up to you, the owner. How much,
what, how often are all within your control. Some

Weighing your dog

dogs are good feeders, some are finicky, funny feeders. Some owners allow their dog to dictate the type of food because the dog refuses anything it does not like. This is nonsense. No healthy dog will starve to death, or even go uncomfortably hungry, if food is available. If the dog has spent 5 years living on English rabbit he'll get an awful shock when the menu changes to ox cheek or tinned food. But he won't starve. Do remember that your dog can be unreasonable, and unreasonably refuse to eat totally adequate food at first. If you were feeding a child he might like ice cream, sausages, baked beans and jelly for breakfast, lunch and tea. Would you provide it?

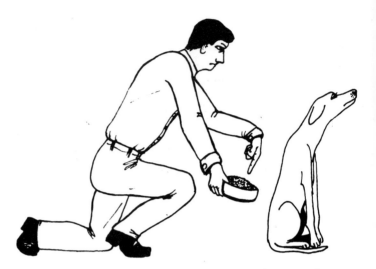

Some owners allow their dogs to dictate the type of food ...

Should you wish to spend more time shopping for your dog than the rest of the family, should you wish to make feeding your dog as expensive as possible, then buy fillet steak, free range chicken, English rabbit by all means and enjoy the feeling of martyrdom that results from being a slave to your pet. But don't feel you have to.

Feeding discipline applies to timing of meals as much as quantity and variety. Some dogs eat what is put in front of them at once and clear their dish. Others take a mouthful and leave the rest for another time so that meal times last all day. Make it clear to your dog, while he is a puppy, that feeding time is of your choosing. Put his food down and if it's not eaten in twenty minutes, take it away. No more until the next feeding time of your choice. No matter how hungry or pleading he looks.

Some dogs are always 'miserable' feeders. They eat well one day, little the next. This is the nature of the beast. If he seems healthy, bright, and cheerful in every respect it's nothing to worry about. If you check his weight and there's no weight loss you've just got that sort of dog and the sooner you stop worrying about it the better.

Vegetables

Vegetables are not necessary for the dog. You can use them in feeding and cooked cabbage, raw or cooked carrot provide useful bulk but hardly any feeding value. They are good slimming aids. Your dog can have a well-filled tummy—full of cabbage and little or no food value from it. Carrots, particularly raw carrots, can be an excellent tit-bit, if you persuade your dog to like them. No danger of too many, no danger of sticky chocolate drops on the carpet.

There's no harm in tit-bits or rewards at any time—except overweight. A chocolate drop, a piece of sweet biscuit will never do any harm to a dog. But a piece of chocolate every day, say 2 oz per week, could well be responsible for 2 oz extra weight per month if the chocolate is an addition to an adequate diet.

If your dog is one of Pharaoh's lean kind you needn't worry about any extras. But few dogs are so fortunate.

Minerals and vitamins

No talk about feeding would be complete without a mention of minerals and vitamins. Mention is all. A good mixed diet of meat and biscuits provides almost all the vitamins and minerals required by the adult dog. Growing puppies of the very big breeds may need extra, but it is wise to consult your vet first. Excess of vitamins or excess of minerals may cause troubles in themselves, just as much as deficiencies of minerals or vitamins. If there is a vitamin deficiency, supplying the particular vitamin will provide a wonderful response. If there's no deficiency, giving extra vitamins is useless—and could be harmful.

Much the same principles apply to 'tonics'. A healthy dog, well fed, doesn't need them. If he's not well, find out why not from your vet, don't just give him a tonic and hope.

Water

Your dog needs food but he also needs fluid. Water should be always available. He'll drink enough. It may not seem much to you but remember that a lot of food contains large amounts of water and he's obtaining some of his fluid requirements this way. Hot weather makes little difference to a dog's drinking. He perspires very little and so loses little extra fluid. Keep water available at all times—let your dog decide how much he needs.

If you notice him drinking a lot more than usual take note of this and if it persists for many days consult your vet. Various dog ailments start with thirst as their first sign.

One still sees yellow lumps of rock sulphur in dogs' drinking bowls. In many cases the sulphur must be older than your dog. Sulphur is totally insoluble in water and the lump of sulphur that your great-grand-mother put in her dog's water bowl will suffice for your dog. It will remain quite unchanged, undissolved and as useless to your dog as to great-grand-mother.

Dogs like milk. Sometimes they like it too much. Once they're semi-adult they don't need milk. But because they like it there is a tendency for them to drink too much, to fill themselves up with this delicious fluid, leaving no room for solid food. The Milk Marketing Board spend a lot of money extolling the virtues of milk as a slimming food. It's 89 per cent water, so be careful that a growing puppy does not go short of solid food because he's so fond of milk. In some few dogs milk is inclined to give diarrhoea— the remedy is simple. Don't give milk, and if he steals the cat's milk then maybe your poor cat has to go without also!

This is a long chapter on a very simple subject. Dog feeding is easy and simple. Some owners of dogs make it complicated and difficult. Don't do this, or you'll lose some of the pleasures of having a dog.

Grooming

Short-haired dogs enjoy a brushing and the coat is cleaned to a certain extent in this way. All other types, from slightly long-haired to very hairy breeds need regular combing as an essential attention. An uncombed dog develops matted hair around the ears, the feet, in fact all over. Pieces of twigs, grass stems, burrs and seeds become tangled in these mats and a smelly, untidy and uncomfortable dog results. It is not sufficient to send your dog to a canine beauty parlour every six months so that he can be stripped or clipped. Every long-haired dog should be kept regularly combed and clean.

But my dog doesn't like being combed ...

'But my dog doesn't like being combed'—neither do many children, though the wise and reasonable parent takes little notice of childish protests. Start using a comb from the word go. Of course there is little to comb on an eight-week-old puppy but you are beginning training. Train him to accept a comb, to accept your will, or maybe even that it is easier to grin and bear it than to argue.

With small- and medium-sized dogs the best place for any grooming—or any other attention for that matter—is on a table; that is, with the dog on a table. Choose a table with a slightly slippery surface that is a convenient height for you. The dog is out of his element; he's a little insecure because there isn't a good grip. You are working at a convenient height and in circumstances within your element. The alternative of the dog on the floor and you on your knees or bent double is making life easy for him and difficult for you.

These rules apply to any handling. You might have to give your dog tablets: you might have to put drops into his eye or ear. If he has been taught that on the table means behaving well, that it's not worth struggling because you always win, if he knows that the one way to end this slightly unpleasant attention is good behaviour, to endure and get it over, then you have saved yourself no end of trouble and ensured that you will be able to give your dog attention and treatments should he need them.

The way to comb

But back to combing. Use a steel comb—plastic ones break. A comb with a handle is easier to use and the leverage of the handle is useful if tangles in the coat have to be sorted out.

Comb through the hair, not just over the top. If there are tangles, use the comb to 'tease' them out a bit at a time; with patience they'll come clear. Ears, feet and the hind end are the most important areas, but don't forget the face.

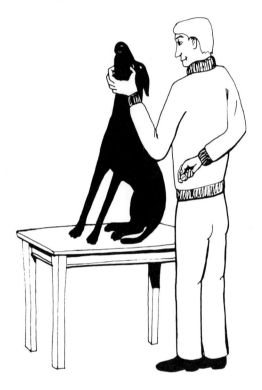

You might have to give your dog tablets . . .

If you own one of the larger dogs, too big to put on a table, you can make a low bench for him. But in any case define some fixed grooming area so that the dog knows that good behaviour and a little patience (on his part) are required here. When it's good weather a low terrace garden wall makes a good grooming place.

Bathing

It is not wrong to bath a dog. It is not necessary to bath most dogs at regular intervals but if any dog is dirty or smelly there is every reason to wash him so that he becomes acceptable in polite company again. If he's itchy or has any skin trouble it is possible that your vet will prescribe some type of medicated bath.

Bathing does remove some of the natural oil from the coat but as it is very unlikely that your dog is going to spend a night out in the rain, the loss of a little of this waterproofing will not matter. If we went back to living in caves we might not wash our own hair quite so often, we would be grateful too for a little grease and grime to keep the damp out.

Use one of the proprietary dog shampoos or one of the standard human hair shampoos. Just as grooming a dog is easier if the dog is off the ground, so is bathing. A draining board is very suitable for small dogs. Fill the sink with tepid to warm water and put the dog on the draining board. Use a plastic jug or beaker to scoop the water over him and lather him while he's on the draining board. When he's wet and soapy all over is the time to put him in the water to rinse. If you try to wash the dog who is up to his middle in water the 'underwater' bits only get wet, not washed, and it's quite possible that you will get wetter than your dog.

Very many people bath the dog in their own bath and seem to manage successfully. There is some difficulty in handling the dog and any owner who is slightly pear-shaped must find kneeling down, while the edge of the bath cuts into his abdomen, a difficult manoeuvre.

After bathing, use old towels to rub him dry, or you can use a hair dryer, but if you do, *concentrate*. Keep the dryer moving so that you do not heat one spot too much and cause a minor burn. After bathing and drying he's back to normal and he will not 'catch cold' if you use normal commonsense behaviour afterwards. Don't bath a dog and then leave him outside in sub-zero temperatures and a cold east wind—but who would?

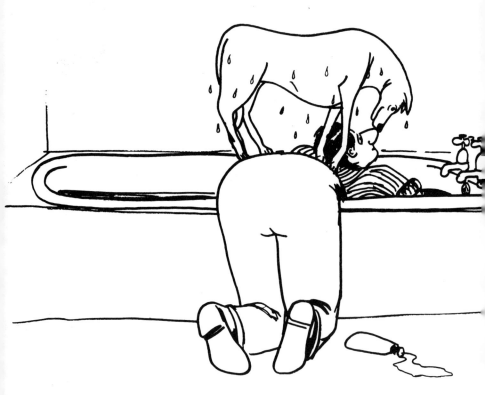

There is some difficulty in handling the dog ...

Other grooming

Some dogs, particularly the hairy-faced kind, tend to get tear stains running from the inside corner of the eye. Slightly excess tears are produced and collect on the hair. When these tears dry they cake and turn brown—dark mahogany brown. Sometimes the owner thinks this is dried blood. It is important to wash the tears away. The mat of hair and dried tear can produce a sore patch which your dog then rubs and enlarges so that it is not long before a very nasty skin lesion results. Washing the tear away with a little pledget of cotton wool, well soaked in warm water, will prevent a sore area developing and make the dog look tidier. Wash away—do not wipe with dry cotton wool and merely smear.

The same brown-coloured staining can be seen on the lower jaw of some white dogs. In this case a 'dribbly' dog has an accumulation of saliva on his whiskers and dried saliva oxidises to turn brown. Again, this should be washed away.

If any dog has diarrhoea—maybe only slightly---faeces can collect on the hair around the tail end. Wash, don't wipe: use soap (gentle toilet soap) and make sure that this end of the dog keeps tidy and non-smelly.

Nails

Nails sometimes need attention. For convenience consider them in two groups. First, the dewclaws. These are the extra nails and pads on the inside of the front legs, and more rarely the back legs—the equivalent of our thumb. Many puppies have them removed at 3 or 4 days old, and it is quite possible your puppy does not own any dewclaws. But if he has, don't worry. Most dogs go through life without the dewclaw needing attention. Sometimes a nail is broken, sometimes the nails overgrow and need cutting—more commonly a problem with the hind dewclaws. It is not possible to give any advice that fits every dewclaw, but it's worth asking your vet—possibly when you take your puppy to visit the surgery for inoculations—about your puppy's particular dewclaws.

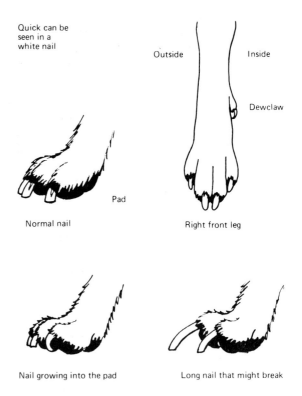

Normal nail

Right front leg

Nail growing into the pad

Long nail that might break

The other nails—of which there are four on each foot—will possibly last the whole of the dog's life without any attention. Nail cutting as a regular procedure is necessary only if the nails do not wear properly. All nails grow, variation is in the extent of wear. If you are a bricklayer, it is unlikely that your nails require much cutting: but if the heaviest thing you handle in your daily work is a sheet of paper, regular manicures are the order of the day. So with your dog. An average weight dog, walking on all sorts of surfaces, keeps his nails well worn. A very light dog living on carpets and well tended lawns quickly develops long nails which need trimming. An old dog taking little exercise might need nails cut late in life. A few dogs have one toe slightly misplaced or twisted and one nail does not wear.

Long nails cause pain only when they grow into a circle and begin to penetrate the pad. Long nails running away from the pad are prone to break because their length makes for leverage, but the long nail does not deform a foot or make your dog flat footed. Rather, the flat footed dog develops long nails.

Training

From the moment he's born your puppy is learning; learning how to cope with life, finding out what he can get away with and what he can't get away with; finding out his place in the scheme of things.

Dogs are 'pack' animals and within the pack there is a very definite pecking order. That is a rather mixed metaphor, but every husband knows the meaning of it!

Your puppy may be the only dog in the house, but he will have that pack state of mind and you and the rest of the family, including the cat, are part of his pack. Within that pack he has to establish his place.

The rest of the family, including the cat, are his 'pack'

Is he to be top dog? You're in for trouble if he is. But if he's not, if he's third, fourth or fifth down the social scale he does not mind. He does not resent it, so long as his place is clear and unchanging. As the hymn by Mrs C. F. Alexander has it:

> 'The rich man in his castle
> The poor man at his gate
> God made them, high or lowly
> And ordered their estate.'

Modern sociological thought has led to omission of this verse from the version usually sung, but your puppy still thinks in this way and is content in his ordered estate!

Once a puppy has established his place in the social order of things he then knows whom to try to please. Every dog likes approval and once he has 'pack' superiors there is pleasure to be had by gaining their approbation.

By now you are probably feeling like most sensible parents feel when exposed to the theories of the more recondite child psychologists or any child psychologist. Be patient! Common sense is returning; theory no more! How to train your puppy. In three words: approval, disapproval and repetition.

Approval is easy with tone of voice, a pat, a ruffle of the coat. The only difficulty is to approve at the right time. If, for example, you've been calling him to come to you for half an hour, he's running round the garden, you want to go out and he finally deigns to come. You still have to congratulate him. He has done as you asked, however slowly. Should you chastise him, he'll associate punishment with final arrival and next time he will stay away longer.

Disapproval must be at the right time; instantly. Owners will often say they smack their dog on his bottom with a piece of rolled up newspaper when he's done something wrong. Poor confused dog. By the time the owner has found a newspaper, ensured it's not today's, rolled it up, found the dog and placed him facing the right direction, it's much too late. The crime is finished and forgotten as far as the puppy is concerned and he just cannot understand the reason for the whack.

A loud bellow at the puppy, a slap with the hand, not to cause agony, but just to bring him up with a jerk, at the instant of wrong-doing is the only way. Two slaps are useless as he doesn't know what the second one is for. All this has nothing to do with formal training. This is just basic training, or discipline. Training to sit, walk at heel, lie, come when called, comes later but one piece of training starts from the word go.

This is toilet training; repetition, habit. Take him out to the same place, same times each day, stay out until he's performed and then approve. *If you catch him* urinating or defecating shout or disapprove in some way. If you only find the resultant mess minutes or hours afterwards it's too late to chastise him. You'll only teach him that it is wrong to be found out.

This sort of repetition, approval and disapproval must go on and on. Even create a crisis in order to solve it. Take food out of his mouth, take his bowl away while he's feeding. This will teach him that you can take it away if you want to and if he trusts you he will realize that the food comes back again.

This sort of early training prevents the development of a dog who bites everyone who approaches his food dish. Your puppy will grow up expecting to obey. Sitting when told, walking at heel, staying on the ground (instead of chairs or jumping on someone's new tights) are all taught by using the same simple principles in the same way time and time again. Please be consistent. Use the same words all the time. 'Sit' must mean sit, 'Down' must not mean sit also.

If you do not want your dog to jump up to greet

people never allow him to do this. If you sometimes accept this 'jumping up' greeting, and then ask your dog to recognize that today you are wearing your dark suit so he must not put muddy paws or white hairs on it, you are being a most unreasonable dog owner—and very bad dog trainer.

... if you do not want your dog to jump up to greet people ...

Fleas and such

A gentleman named Augustus De Morgan once wrote:

> 'Great fleas have little fleas
> Upon their back to bitum
> And little fleas have lesser fleas
> And so ad infinitum.'

Maybe that's amusing poetry but it is not accurate in scientific terms. Nevertheless fleas can get on dogs' backs and 'bitum'; uncomfortable for the dog, uncomfortable maybe for the owner, and a socially unacceptable situation. All dogs do not have to have fleas. Fleas are not normally caught from birds, rats, mice or hedgehogs. Almost every infection is from another dog or cat. Dogs do not breed fleas. The only animals that can breed a flea are two other fleas.

There are many distinct species of fleas. Two species, the dog flea and the cat flea, concern us, but as these fleas can also live on the human owner they should be treated seriously. Human fleas are a different species again but will rarely live on dogs. Poultry fleas, rabbit fleas and all the myriad other fleas are of no concern to the dog.

Sometimes the owner of a dog gets bitten by fleas. Very uncomfortable, but no real harm results. Usually young girls are the victims. One may console them by suggesting that the flea is very particular, that only a very delicate skin would be bitten, but this is of little help. So take fleas rather seriously and stop an infection before it starts. Fleas breed away from the dog, the adult fleas hop off and find a warm, dusty place and there lay eggs. These eggs hatch into larvae and then develop into young fleas. These immature fleas are capable of living for many months feeding

off dirt and debris. They only go in search of a dog
or cat as adult fleas.

By now you may well be scratching, but it's in
a good cause. If you understand how fleas live you'll be
more successful in keeping them away.

Killing a flea is easy, getting at it is more difficult.
Most proprietary flea powders made for dogs are
effective and safe if you can reach the flea. But fleas
live on the skin, not the hair, and with a long-haired
dog, penetration through the coat to the skin is difficult. Fleas live on the dog's underneath as well as his
back; so often a dog's back is well dusted with
powder, and his tummy is ignored. The fleas emigrate
'down under' and live happily ever after. Bathing
with a suitable insecticidal soap or shampoo is more
effective in that the lather penetrates the hair and the
fleas on the skin are exposed. One single treatment
will not get rid of fleas, especially if they have been
on the dog for a few weeks before you start. Inevitably some will have left him and set up house, laying
eggs somewhere around the dog's box, or in the
cracks in the floor boards. You can use your dog as
a vacuum cleaner. When the fleas grow up and reach
the dog, kill them by routine dusting or bathing.

It's possible to buy flea collars, plastic impregnated
with a substance which will kill fleas, and have your
dog wear one all the time. They seem to work very
well and, except for the very few dogs that are allergic
to them, are very safe. If you have toddlers in the
house, it might be unwise to use these collars. If the
child hangs on to the dog's flea collar with his hot
sticky hand and then eats his lollipop with the same
hand, it could be that when he licks his fingers he's
getting a dose of flea killer, which is obviously not
a good thing.

When you own more than one animal treat them
all for fleas at the same time and if your dog is great

friends with your neighbour's dog, there will be neighbourly fleas also.

All this may seem to be making a lot about fleas but they are increasing on both cats and dogs. Quite possibly the affluent society is responsible for this increase. More central heating, more fitted carpets mean more nice, warm and dusty areas under the carpets and make for more flea maternity homes. A little trouble, a little care so that the first flea on your dog is removed quickly and you'll never have problems.

Lice are other fellow travellers. These live on the dog all the time and breed on the dog. They are usually seen on the ears especially on long, hairy-eared dogs. Lice are easy to kill with medicated shampoos. Bath the dog at least twice at 10-day intervals. The first bath kills the lice, but not their eggs. The second one kills the newly hatched lice before they have grown old enough to lay eggs. There are many other causes of itching in dogs. A dog should not scratch other than very occasionally. If your dog's itchy and you cannot find fleas or lice, take him to your vet. An itchy dog is uncomfortable, he loses rest and you feel 'scratchy'. Almost every type of skin trouble can be considerably eased by treatment and most can be cured. You'll hear stories about Mrs Somebody's dog that had to be put to sleep because it had skin trouble. Very, very often the true story was that Mrs Somebody was not prepared to take very much trouble in treating the dog. Maybe she didn't really want him anyhow and skin trouble was a conscience-saving excuse for disposing of an unwanted animal.

Worms—like boys—come in all sizes—the biggest not necessarily being the most troublesome.

More than 50 different worms can live in the dog; many are rare, some are nearly extinct in this country, some are serious, many do little or no harm to the dog. This is not a textbook of parasitology so most of these worms need not be mentioned. Those that do happen and do concern you are of two main groups.

Tape worms often cause more consternation to the owner than harm to the dog. The commonest of them is nearly harmless. It's called Dipylidium caninum—which doesn't really help anyone but does allow us to talk about its fascinating life cycle.

The segments of this worm appear on the dog's motions or even just crawl out of his anus. They're little, flattened, cream-coloured objects, the size and shape of a small melon seed. They wriggle about—and this is about the only tape worm that does move. These segments are full of eggs, and separate from the end of the whole tape worm. The segments dry up to look like little seeds on the hair of the back end of the dog.

As segments these are totally harmless to dogs, to you, to anything. Before further development of the worm can take place the egg must be eaten by a larval flea. The worm then develops in the flea and a dog can only be infected by swallowing a flea containing the worm—so that is another reason for keeping your dog free of fleas.

No one likes to see the worms leaving their dog—that's a good reason for treating him if you see worms. But in many cases it's your aesthetic senses that are offended; the dog and the worm are quite happy living together.

Among the other tape worms is one, happily fairly rare, that can cause disease in humans. This is a tiny worm: too small to be seen with the naked eye, called Echinococcus granulosus. The adult worm lives in the dog and like every other tape worm the eggs are

passed out with the dog's faeces. These eggs, if they
get onto grass that is eaten by sheep will develop into
a large fluid-filled cyst in the lungs or liver of the
sheep. Within this bag of fluid are tiny immature
worms ready to develop if the sheep is eaten by a dog.
These cysts can kill the sheep and this worm is important in areas where sheep and dogs are in close contact.
Should a human being swallow the worm eggs—and
he can do so by stroking an infected dog which has
the eggs on the coat—the cyst can develop and cause
very serious illness in man.

In some parts of South Wales the sheep come into
the valleys, and a wandering dog may eat part of a
dead sheep which has been infected with the cyst and
so the dog develops the tape worm. New Zealand,
with its very important sheep industry, takes this
worm very seriously and any dog being exported
to New Zealand has to be wormed by a veterinary
surgeon so that no possible traces of Echinococcus
remain.

Don't get too worried—the worm does exist, it
does cause some serious human illness but only in a
very few people. Good sensible dog keeping, good
hygiene when you handle your pet will keep trouble
away.

Round worms. The other main group of worms are
the round worms, round in cross-section. The commonest is called Toxocara canis, a wiry looking
worm some 2–6 inches long, pale cream/brown in
colour often curling like a spring into a circle. This
worm has a less than simple life-cycle too, but only
in one host. The eggs are passed out of the dog, too
small to be seen by the naked eye, and after a period
of time outside develop into infective larvae. If the
infective egg is eaten by another dog the eggs hatch
in the intestines and the tiny larvae burrow through

the intestine wall, into the blood stream. They travel through the liver, then into the lungs, up the wind-pipe, then they are swallowed and go back to the in-testine where they were hatched. A sort of Cook's tour with no apparent purpose.

However, this journey has a number of important consequences. If these larvae are travelling about in a pregnant bitch they can enter a puppy before birth. If they are travelling about when a dog is wormed the worms will be killed but not the migrating larvae, so for really effective control of round worm two wormings are necessary at about 14-day intervals. The first to kill the adult worms, the second to kill the larvae when they have returned to the intestine but before they're old enough to produce more eggs.

The third, rare consequence is that young children can get troubles from the larvae. If a young child swallows the eggs, the larvae will hatch and enter the blood stream. Because the larvae are in a strange, and to them unsuitable host, most of them die, although their presence can be detected by medical tests. A few may continue to live and can arrive in the brain or at the back of the eye. In humans this infestation is known as larva migrans. It is very rare; keep the risk in proportion. Thousands of children mix with pets and suffer no ills. Motor cars, bicycles, fires, injure and kill in one month more children than have suffered larva migrans infection since time began, but it can and it does occur, and keeping your puppy free of roundworm and insisting on basic hygiene by your children will prevent your being concerned with this problem.

Keep worms in proportion too. Reading some of the 'horror comic' literature produced by people whose income is derived from selling worm medi-cines can give you the impression that if your dog has a broken leg a worm dose will cure it. Bad health, bad coat, bad temper, coughs, itches, underweight, overweight are all blamed on the poor old worm. Mostly nonsense, but there may be some truth deeply buried.

If you are worried about worms, or if you find a worm from your dog, take both dog and worm to your vet. In particular, take the worm. It is important to identify it, both to assess the importance and to prescribe the correct treatment. Descriptions are usually graphic but rarely accurate enough to be useful. On one occasion a frantic message was received from the only English-speaking member of a Liberian ship, manned by a Turkish crew, that snakes were coming out of a dog's mouth. On arrival the snakes were produced—ordinary round worms—and the language barrier overcome on sight. One hears descriptions from native Britons that are no more accurate.

When you take a worm, wrap it, or put it in a polythene bag. This morning's tiny worm, placed in tissue paper is a dried up nothing by evening surgery.

You may be warned about worms but you haven't seen any. Don't just make your dog rattle by filling him full of all types of worm tablets. A sample of faeces can be examined microscopically, and if worms or worm eggs are there they can be found. If nothing is found in one sample it does not necessarily mean that your dog has no worms. It means nothing was found in that sample, but if two or three samples reveal no eggs or worms it's fairly certain that there's nothing in the dog. Instead of sampling, routine worming for round worms (Toxocara) is good, responsible pet keeping. Even if the odd worm is doing no harm at all to your dog you are playing your part in reducing the tiny risk of human infection. Every 6 months is a reasonable interval and your vet can supply worm doses which will be effective and cause no discomfort at all to your dog.

Simple troubles

Common things occur commonly—a very good maxim for every diagnostician, amateur archaeologist or stamp collector, not to mention the dog owner. Simple troubles occur commonly and simple explanations abound for these troubles. If your dog scratches he might have a flea. Look for one, and only if you cannot find one, start to think of other things.

There are a number of recurrent troubles worth mentioning. To start from the front end, ears are a major source of trouble, especially in the floppy-eared breeds. Sheer lack of ventilation frequently causes this and lack of combing predisposes to it. Some spaniels' ears are so heavy and matted that one wonders how the dog manages to hold his head up with such an excess of hair. One also wonders how the owners live with the resultant smell. Good regular grooming of ear flaps is essential, but that's about all that is essential in routine ear care.

The whole design of the ear is one of folds and obstructions to keep out foreign bodies. Scraping around the ear every day to 'clean it' only irritates. The ear's natural reaction to an irritation is to produce wax as a protection. The more you clean, the more the ear produces wax and the more you have to clean.

If your dog is unconscious of his ears, if he doesn't scratch, if they look reasonably clean, *leave well alone.* On the other hand, if he's shaking his head, scratching his ears or they smell badly, then something is wrong and you need a veterinary surgeon to diagnose the trouble. So many different things can cause trouble in ears that no one treatment is correct for all causes. Which leads us to 'canker'. A horrible word which sounds vaguely like cancer and frightens all owners. All 'canker' means is a bad ear, rather like 'tummy

ache' when you might have eaten too many strawberries or you might be having a baby. Indigestion
medicine might help a surfeit of strawberries, but not
the baby. 'Canker' lotion might help one ear but not
the next.

Sickness is common in dogs, sometimes a symptom
of serious disease, sometimes nothing more than
over-eating. A bitch will sometimes vomit food to
feed her weaning puppies. If your dog is sick just once
and appears well in every other way, this is of little
consequence, but continuous vomiting can be a sign
of serious trouble or can, in itself, cause illness by
dehydration. A word of warning here. Never let a
vomiting dog drink too much *at one drink*. Having
been sick, he's thirsty, he has a good drink—too much
for an upset stomach—and woosh, out it comes again,
plus a little bit of stomach content. He feels even
thirstier, has another drink, vomits again and this can
proceed until he's seriously short of fluid. This dog
needs very tiny drinks to replace his fluid without
making him sick. A teaspoon of water that he retains
and absorbs is more use than a pint he vomits.

So, for any vomiting dog, give tiny drinks at half-
hour intervals, and take his water bowl away. Water
is best too, as milk nearly always makes things worse.
Any sickness that's repeated needs to be properly
diagnosed, necessitating a journey to your vet.

Still at the head we consider the eyes. Any eye
trouble is potentially serious. We have only 2 eyes,
and they're delicate organs and damage tends to be
permanent. A watery eye, a pusy eye—find out and
have proper treatment. Don't take your neighbour's
advice, no matter how well intended.

Travelling backwards we reach the middle: milk
and the bitch. Each and every bitch has a false pregnancy about 6–10 weeks after every heat, unless, of
course, she has a real pregnancy, false pregnancy

being normal otherwise. The ovaries behave in the same way after heat whether the bitch is pregnant or not, whether she's been mated or not. The hormones that cause development of the udder and milk production are always present 6–8 weeks after heat.

Thus, a little milk is often present and sometimes these hormones cause psychological upsets and the bitch behaves as if she's having or has puppies. She'll take herself to bed, make a nest, tear up furniture or cushions for puppies she's not even conceived. She'll take toys to bed with her and nurse them, sometimes become very possessive of her teddy bear or rag doll.

The signs of false pregnancy are usually so slight that only a very observant owner sees them, or just thinks that his bitch is a little subdued. Even when extreme behaviour occurs the bitch is only overdoing the normal although treatment is sometimes indicated to reduce her considerable distress and worry. But it's still not a disease, it's just overdoing a normal happening.

Mating won't cure it, except for the one time that she's pregnant. If false pregnancies distress your bitch after every heat, neutering is the permanent remedy.

At the rear end of every dog are two little glands that can be a source of nuisance. These are the anal glands, one either side of the anus and just beneath it. They are scent glands which normally fill and empty. In a percentage of dogs they just don't empty, and if they overfill, the dog has an acute consciousness of his rear end. He knows he's got a tail and shows it either by rubbing his bottom along the ground— 'skating' or 'tobogganing'—or by suddenly turning around and biting or licking in his tail region, behaving just as if someone had stuck a pin in him.

The glands can be emptied by squeezing and, once emptied, usually go on normally for weeks or months. It's never possible to predict when or if they will get overfull again. Rather like the drains, they get blocked, but if they're cleared you never know when or if they'll block again.

Back to the glands. If they're left full an infection can develop and a painful abscess. If the filling is recurrent, it's possible to remove them surgically and the troubles will never happen again.

One more rear end trouble, very simple, very obvious, and yet some owners never see it in time. Faeces matted around the anus, sometimes a great mass as big as an orange, stinking, and a dog with a very sore bottom from scalding. In extreme cases in the summer, maggots get into this mess and real troubles start. Again, the 'hairy dog' suffers. Basically it's neglect on the part of the owner, so if your dog is uncomfortable behind and smelly, at least have a look. You might achieve a remarkable improvement with soap and water.

Silly accidents

Quite a proportion of emergency work in veterinary practice consists of 'silly' accidents. Incidents which are not necessarily fatal, or even serious, but which cause distress and panic to both dog and owner.

It's worth mentioning as many as possible because they are nearly all avoidable and if you know what could happen you'll avoid the situation. And as every preacher knows, the word will spread and more will be saved. Let's group them as follows:

Those affecting the head end, from the neck forwards. This is the largest group probably because dogs use their mouths for much more than eating.

Sticks can be dangerous. Throwing a stick for a dog can lead to serious injury when the stick sticks (sorry about that) in the ground and an over-excited dog runs onto it with his mouth wide open, driving the stick into the roof of the mouth or through the tissue alongside the tongue. In extreme cases a penetration right down the neck can occur and a piece of stick twelve inches long is removed, buried in the neck. So *no sticks*. A block of wood, say 12″ by 2″ by 2″ is safe—or nearly so—but don't hit the dog with it.

Another stick one—much less serious but often spectacular—is the piece of stick, tree root or bone that gets jammed across the roof of the mouth between the back teeth.

Often a dog digging cuts off a piece of tree root that fits tightly across the roof of the mouth, or it may be a piece of bone, especially a rib bone that can be cut to size.

If you think about it the roof of the mouth is V-shaped and the bone or stick fits across the V (see diagram).

Pushing the bone or stick backwards, to the wider part, releases it immediately but almost every owner when presented with this problem attempts to pull the offending piece, this results in a frantic dog, frantic owner and the bone or stick jammed tighter. Some hardworking veterinary surgeon is disturbed from his Sunday afternoon nap—all these silly accidents have a predilection for Sunday afternoons—and unless the dog is very difficult and has to be anaesthetized even

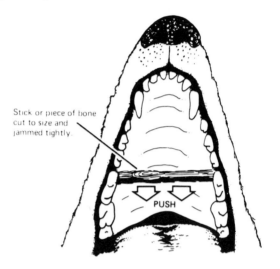

Stick or piece of bone cut to size and jammed tightly.

PUSH

to open his mouth, pushes the offending object backwards, and in a matter of seconds dog is happy and owner feels relieved but embarrassed that he hadn't thought of the obvious action.

'Things' can get stuck between and on the teeth. The usual reaction of the dog is salivation and frantic pawing at this mouth. These 'things' can vary from a caramel—which time and his saliva will solve—to pieces of bone; sometimes the vertebra (piece of backbone) of a rabbit or fish becomes impaled on one of the back teeth, acts as a wedge and the dog cannot close his mouth. This incident happens in little dogs and even more often in the cat if canine readers will forgive this mention of the Auld Enemy.

Even newspaper can be a source of trouble. On one occasion a little West Highland dog was seen unable to open his mouth. He had been chewing newspaper and wet newspaper had swollen between his front teeth—top and bottom—and jammed them tightly together so that he could not separate them.

Most of these incidents happen to the active bored dog who has to find something to do like the 'Just William' type younger brother: when William canine or human is unusually quiet, 'good' and occupied find out what he's doing and tell him not to.

Still at the mouth, but not stopping there, dogs swallow needles. It's not the actual needle that attracts them, it's the piece of thread left in the needle. Embroiderers beware, unthread your needles.

When a needle is swallowed it may lodge either in the root of the tongue or the pharynx—then the dog paws at his mouth, salivates and has some difficulty swallowing, and it's possible to see the thread lying on the surface of the tongue. If the needle does not penetrate in the mouth area it almost always passes through the dog and becomes stuck at the other end, the anus. A very uncomfortable dog is straining to pass a motion and squealing as the needle pricks him. Again there is often a thread to be seen hanging out.

At either end *don't pull the thread.* The dog must be anaesthetized and the thread is an extremely useful guideline to the needle. Without the thread one is looking for the proverbial haystack needle.

Similarly, take care when fishing. Fish hooks have to be removed from dogs' lips, nostrils and eyelids. Cast carefully.

Travelling backwards—dog-wise—we come to the ears. One near accident situation which distresses dogs every summer is the grass seed in the ear. One grass is the offender—wild barley—which has seeds with sharp prickles. This is a town grass, a wasteland grass, and troubles start about the end of June when the seeds are ripe. The prickles get on to the dog's coat, on to the inside of the ear flap. Spaniels, with their large hairy ear flaps, are especially susceptible. Then the prickle goes into the ear canal and causes acute irritation and pain. Often an anaesthetic is necessary to remove it, but attention to the coat could have stopped trouble before it started. Comb the prickles out before they have reached the ear canal and clip the hair on the inside of the ear flap so that there's no anchorage for the seed on the first stage of the journey.

These grass seeds will also get into the feet and penetrate the skin between the toes causing an abscess. If not removed, the grass seed will travel under the skin and so produce a chain of abscesses up the leg as far as the elbow. Nasty. Again prevention is easy. Clip the hair between the toes in summer and the seed cannot begin its journey.

Our journey around the dog has now diverted to the feet. Silly, simple things happen here. One of the silliest is the dog who gets the clip from his lead caught in the web of the foot. The web is a thin layer of skin, partly joining the toes, and provides a suitable anchorage for the clip part of the lead. This happens to the dog who carries his lead, the clip part that you fasten to his collar drags on the ground and suddenly it's fastened to his foot. Dog goes frantic—so does owner—and the vet has to anaesthetize the dog and usually cut the spring clip off the lead to release him. There's no damage to the dog, the clip is merely fixed onto the web, not into it, so no cuts, no blood, lots of panic. If your dog must carry a lead, find an old one with no metal clip on the end. That one is his, you keep the proper one.

Feet get cut, and when they are cut they bleed most spectacularly. Usually big heavy dogs cut their feet. The tiny, light footed 'Twinkletoed' dog isn't heavy enough. He can tread on a piece of glass but he's so light footed that it doesn't cut him. The larger, heavy footed dogs—Boxers in particular, the sort of dog who makes the house shake when he walks through the hall—are prone to this. Blood is everywhere. In fact the amount of blood lost is not very great but blood is like milk—it goes a long way. Drop a bottle of milk and you'd think a cow had burst; a couple of tablespoons of blood and the place looks like a slaughterhouse.

If this happens to your dog apply a tight bandage around the foot and well up the leg. If this has no other benefit, it keeps you and your car fairly blood-free during your journey to the vet's surgery.

Nails get broken. When they do they irritate. Rather like yours. Not much more serious either, but the nail is often only partially broken and the broken bit hangs on. Every time the dog puts his foot down the broken piece traps the quick of the nail and hurts him. He licks at the offending nail. Once the broken bit is removed it heals in a day or so, although an anti-biotic injection might be necessary to prevent infection developing.

That's the head end and legs. The rest of the dog also gets into minor troubles. Things on the coat. Oil, paint, turps, petrol, creosote. Any of these things must be washed off quickly. Lots and lots of soapy water. Turpentine and petrol will blister the skin badly and must never be used to remove paint. The cure is many times more dangerous than the trouble. However 'Swarfega' seems quite safe and the oily dog may be cleaned with this, as you would your own hands.

Things get on the coat ...

Rubber bands cause problems—more often in cats but also in small dogs. Someone—one hopes young children only—puts elastic bands around the legs, the neck or the tail. The band cuts into the skin and of course produces an open wound. The rubber can penetrate a quarter of an inch or more through the skin, and when it does it's quite difficult to find and often needs an anaesthetic to handle the area which is very sensitive—and no wonder.

Lots of other silly things happen but hopefully you'll remember some of this and your dog will avoid the trouble resulting from a moment's thoughtlessness.

Serious accidents

Motor cars and dogs do not mix—at least not when they are both on the same piece of road. The serious accident that can happen to your dog is being 'run over'. In fact, the dog is rarely run over, but he is hit hard by a very solid object and anything from trivial bruising to instant death can result.

No dog is safe on the highway unless he's on a lead, with a wide-awake owner on the other end of the lead. You yourself can step into the path of a car and think that you can make it across the road, but fail, due to the momentary inattention of the driver. In spite of the claims of some animal lovers, man's intelligence and anticipation is more advanced than the dog's—so if *you* can get into trouble on the road, so can your dog.

There are three main groups of injury received if your dog should be run over. The scraping, burning type, where the dog suffers his damage from violent contact with the road. He may be badly bruised where the car hits him, but the more spectacular injury is from gravel grazing and 'burning' on the road surface. This is very painful, as the skin has been scraped away and healing is slow. Very often, one or more toes are broken. The owner panics, and the dog is in a lot of pain, but he survives. Stitching is required, with dressing of open wounds, but he does survive, with a wiser owner resolved to use a lead in the future.

Broken bones—usually legs, and the commonest is the femur or thigh bone. Any of the other bones may be broken, and of course the back, pelvis, skull or ribs are at risk. Modern orthopaedic surgery makes it possible to repair some very extensive injuries. Open surgery, rather than plaster of Paris is the method

chosen on most occasions and this means putting a
stainless steel pin down the centre of a broken bone,
or joining the fragments together with a metal plate
not unlike the carpentry that is involved in repair-
ing granny's old rocking chair. Results are excellent
and the majority of broken bones can be restored to
totally normal use.

Internal injuries are serious and often fatal. The
heavy impact of a motor car on a dog's abdomen can
rupture the liver, the spleen and the large arteries to
the intestine as well. Massive bleeding into the
abdomen can cause rapid death. There are often no
external signs on the dog and every veterinary surgeon has been asked to post mortem dogs, 'found
dead' and 'possibly poisoned', a large number of
which prove to have been hit by a car. The dogs have
been hit in the road, their spleen has been ruptured,
but in the five or so minutes before death they have
managed to reach home.

If the last few pages haven't made you ultra-
cautious with your dog and if he still happens to meet
with a motor accident, what should you do? Take
him to your veterinary surgeon. Do note—*take
him*. There is little that can usefully be done at
home. X-ray facilities might be needed as well as
operative facilities, oxygen and fluid drips. All these
facilities are at your vet's surgery. They're not in your
kitchen.

Always telephone your veterinary surgeon first.
All practising veterinary surgeons have arrangements
to deal with emergency cases that occur during 'anti-
social' hours, but this does not mean that there is a
vet sitting at his surgery waiting for your dog to be
run over. Phone first so that if a vet has to be called
from his home to the surgery he can begin travelling
when you start off.

If you have a little dog, put him in a box or basket.

The cardboard box that last week's groceries came in might do. You can then carry box and dog—so if there is a little bleeding or he has another accident on the way, the car seat will not be damaged, and he will be more comfortable.

For a big dog, an old strong blanket makes a very useful stretcher if he cannot walk. Place the doubled blanket next to the dog and roll him on to it. Two people then take two corners each of the blanket and lift the dog slung in his hammock. If you're putting him into a car, one person crawls backwards through the car by the backdoors and leaves the dog on the blanket, so that when you come to take him out of the car, he's still on his stretcher.

Collars and leads are useful with the injured dog. To pick him up, put one hand in the collar, forward towards his ears, and the other hand under his tummy. Control of the head means you cannot get bitten.

The first major decision you will have to make if your dog gets badly injured is whether to have him treated or put to sleep. Try to be as dispassionate as possible and ask your vet for his views. The decision must be yours and no one can make it for you but every vet will help you as much as he can.

Pain alone is not the criterion. Every dog that's been hit by a motor car is suffering some pain. What really matters is how reasonable it is to ask him to suffer it. A young dog with a broken leg will have a week or so of pain, not so much from the broken leg as from all the bruises that accompany it, yet he may go on to have ten or twelve years of totally pain-free life. This is surely a fair exchange. A very old dog is not going to recover as quickly as the young one, and if he's approaching the end of his allotted span one is reluctant to see him uncomfortable and unhappy for two or three weeks during what is left

of his life. It is your decision but these are some of
the factors you should consider.

There is another group of dog accidents that pose
problems of their own—the injured stray dog without a collar or with a collar but no name found by
a Good Samaritan who may be you. What should
you do? Take the dog into your house, car or at least
restrain him in some way so that he does not panic
and run off. The Local Authority and the Police have
an obligation to provide necessary care and attention
to any stray dog for seven days. Most take their re-
sponsibility seriously. Some few do not. So contact
the Police. They may have arrangements in their area.
If you are able and willing, take the dog to a
veterinary surgeon, *after contacting the Police*, as some
distraught owner may be phoning the Police to know
if they have found his dog. The R.S.P.C.A. might
also help, but please do not just phone from the next
call box and say 'there's an injured dog in the road'.
Every veterinary surgeon has been out on these calls
and found no dog. Lots of time is wasted and most
important of all, an injured dog is lying somewhere untreated.

Poisons and poisoning

'Could it be poison?' This is a question that every veterinary surgeon hears many times each week. Usually the answer is no, but poisoning does occur in all animals, not least in the active, curious, young puppy who wants to sample everything.

The question is often posed when a dog is vomiting. Dogs can vomit very easily and sickness may be a symptom of dozens of separate ailments. Whole books have been written about 'the vomiting dog' and the diagnosis of the cause of vomiting is a problem in itself. A poisoned dog often is sick and saves his own life by ejecting the poison.

If at any time you suspect that your dog has just swallowed poison, make him vomit. A piece of common washing soda the size of your thumb nail will do this. Give it to him like a pill and within five minutes, 'hey presto'. Salt water is not a satisfactory emetic. It rarely works and can lead to salt poisoning.

Emetics work well if he's just swallowed a poison, say ten minutes before. It's out of the stomach and the dog, before any damage is done.

What poisonings do occur? Very many substances are poisonous, but those that cause most trouble are:
Rat and mouse poison
Slug pellets
Granny's pills
More rarely: strychnine—malicious poisoning, or its illegal use for fox killing.
lead—from chewing old painted woodwork.
arsenic—from weedkillers and malicious poisoning.
There are many other poisonous substances, but the above are the most common.

Rat and mouse poison. One of these, alpha
chloralose, which is used for warfarin-resistant mice,
is the commonest rodent poison involved. It is a very
good, very humane mouse poison—it works like a
simple anaesthetic, and the mouse goes into a deep
sleep. Because the mouse is such a tiny animal, it loses
a lot of heat and dies from cold while anaesthetized.
This poison does not work very well in hot weather
or in centrally heated buildings. If the mouse curls up
asleep by a heating pipe it wakes up a day later with
nothing more than a thick head.

Dogs are much bigger animals, so if they take this
poison they are only anaesthetized to a greater or
lesser degree.

A small dog getting a big dose goes out like a light
and stays totally unconscious, but if he's kept warm,
there's a very good prospect of total recovery.

With a smaller dose, or a bigger dog, full anaesthesia does not occur—only a state between drunken-
ness and anaesthetic excitement. The dog may lose
the use of his back legs, lurch about, sometimes get
very excited and react violently if touched or even
spoken to. Again all symptoms will pass off but the
dog must be kept warm and it's wise to keep him in
a cage so that he doesn't lurch into the road, the fire
or knock over Aunt Agatha's Sèvres vase.

The other rodent poisons can be more dangerous.
There are a number of them and in spite of the op-
timistic labels on packets and of the bland assurances of rodent operators, they are dangerous to pet
animals.

One very useful thing you can do is to make certain that if you buy poisons you follow instructions,
place baits where the most enterprising puppy cannot reach them and *keep the packet*. If rodent control
people are using baits in your area insist that they
write down the name of the bait they are using, for

you to keep, and that they place the baits in safe places.

Should your dog, or cat, be unfortunate enough to eat rodent poison, it is of immense help to your vet if you can tell him what poison has been used, either from the packet if you bought it or the paper you insisted on having.

There are antidotes, but unless one knows the poison the choice of antidote is well-nigh impossible.

Slug pellets made of metaldehyde are lethal to dogs if eaten in any quantity, so be very careful with these.

If you are a keen gardener you must be a slug hater and you can use slug killers if you follow certain rules.

Liquid slug killers are safer, in that the amount on any one leaf is much less than a pellet. If you use pellets, spread them very thinly, one here, one there. The slugs will find the pellets. There's no need to make a great heap of pellets for the slug to fall over and break his neck.

An even safer method is to place the pellets under a large flagstone, raised an inch or so above the ground. Your puppy can't reach them and the slugs and snails are attracted to the moist, cool area underneath the flagstone. You can use this idea for rodent baits also. Store your slug baits and any other such dangerous delicacies out of *everyone's* way. Puppies, cats and children are at risk so take care.

Granny's pills and all medicines are nowadays usually supplied in child-proof containers, which work well in protecting children (so long as you remember to put the lid back) but an active puppy will chew up container, tablets, instructions and all.

If anything like this happens, phone your doctor before setting out to visit your vet. If you know what the tablet contained, what strength it was and how

many were left, you can be of immense help to your
vet, and your dog. It may be that the tablets are harmless, but the vet can only decide this after knowing
exactly what the tablet contains. 'They're green ones
for her nerves', doesn't really help.

Dogs are quite unselective in their tastes. On at least
one occasion a veterinary surgeon was telephoned in
the early hours of the morning by a man who would
disclose neither name nor address, nor bring his dog

The dog had eaten cannabis

to the surgery. The dog had eaten cannabis. It was suggested that the dog should be vomited using washing soda, but the end of this story remains a mystery.

Most practices have received the frantic phone call from the lady whose dog has eaten a quantity of 'the Pill'. What will happen? We can predict a happy event for the dog. No harm appears to result.

Serious troubles

Motor car accidents account for a lot of the serious troubles of the dog but there are diseases and illness as well.

The curse of dogdom is distemper—and if you are a responsible owner inoculation and regular boosters prevent your dog falling victim to this disease.

The other virus infection, hepatitis, and the bacterial infections of liver and kidneys, leptospiroses, are similarly avoidable by inoculations, but some troubles cannot be prevented.

Pyometra is a common infection of the uterus in the middle-aged bitch. Because of the unusual heat cycle of the bitch this is a problem peculiar to canines. You might remember a mention of false pregnancies in an earlier chapter on simple troubles. Pyometra is a serious complication that occurs during the false pregnancy period.

Because the ovaries and uterus behave as if pregnancy had occurred after every heat, the uterus gets ready to receive the newly fertilized eggs. In the bitch the fertilized egg is not attached to the uterus wall until about ten days after fertilization. During this ten-day period it has to be fed and a lymph-like substance called 'uterine milk' is produced to nourish the puppy-to-be. At the same time the lining of the uterus thickens to prepare itself to receive the young embryo. When pyometra develops this process goes on to excess. Too much uterine milk is produced, too much thickening of the lining of the uterus occurs, and a grossly enlarged uterus full of evil-smelling pus results. The uterine milk is a highly nutritious medium for any passing bacteria and so a very nasty, potentially fatal infection results.

In the majority of cases operation to remove uterus

and ovaries is the usual treatment. While it is sometimes possible to treat this infection medically, results are not good and in any case the whole situation can recur at the next heat.

Operation results are good—they're not perfect, but should your bitch be unfortunate enough to develop this infection, trust your vet and take his advice. Probably two bitches out of five get pyometra as they reach middle age, the vast majority can be operated upon to live contentedly and normally to old age.

Various growths can constitute another set of serious troubles. It is no part of this book to discuss the various types and sorts of growths that can occur in the dog. Sufficient to say they are legion. The vast majority are non-malignant, the vast majority are painless. The vast majority are operable.

Trust your vet, ask your vet at an early stage. The small, harmless growth might be operable now and it might be a simple operation. If you procrastinate for a year or so it could be a much more serious operation, it could be no longer operable.

It could also be that the best treatment of all is to do nothing. Remember, if there is a small growth somewhere, if your dog is twelve years old, sheer senility could claim him before the lump ever began to cause him even slight discomfort. Remember, your dog does not worry about what might happen. Maybe you do. He's luckier.

Breeding

Earlier we talked about the pros and cons of dog or bitch and the advantages of neutering a bitch if you do not wish to breed from her.

If you've got a bitch, and she's not neutered—what about breeding?

Let the bitch have a litter of puppies only if you want her to have puppies—either because you want to make pin money (you won't) or—and this is a very good reason—because you feel it would be interesting and instructive for the children in the family.

There is no benefit to the bitch in breeding from her. Like all 'doggery' there are a number of old wives' tales about breeding: that a litter of puppies will prevent a bitch getting cancer, getting pyometra (an infection of the uterus). Like all old wives' tales, there could be a grain of truth in them since a bitch that breeds regularly—that is a litter most years—does appear to have fewer of these troubles. But this cannot be translated into one litter when a bitch is, say, 2 years old, preventing troubles when she's 10. The uterus hasn't got that sort of memory, and any idea that the bitch will feel 'fulfilled' after parenthood is anthropomorphism at its worst. So, if you decide to breed from your bitch, do so because *you* want her to have a litter of puppies.

You've decided—what next? It is conventional to wait until the second or third heat, when the bitch is between 15 months and 2 years old. Why this convention has developed is difficult to ascertain; one could well contend that Nature, who has arranged these things for rather a long time, would not let a bitch come on heat unless all was ready and suitable for breeding. Still, let's stick to convention and decide on second or third heat, according to the time of year.

Spring-born puppies are best and easiest, so the spring heat of February or March with puppies born April or May for choice. The puppies have summer to grow up in, and when they're 6 or 8 weeks old there's an even chance that the weather will be dry and warm so that they can spend time out in the garden.

Puppies born in September/October have to face winter early in life and 24 tiny feet paddling in and out of the garden in a wet November will try the patience of the saint that you are.

Nothing in this world is as simple as it seems, however, and the autumn puppies are often easier to sell—as Christmas presents—than the one that's ready for his new home in July when all the potential new owners are thinking of summer holidays. But spring puppies have advantages and Christmas, with all the attendant excitement, is not the best time to introduce a puppy to his new home.

You will, of course, have to find a potential father for these puppies, and think of this in plenty of time especially if you have one of the less common breeds. It may be that the breeder of your bitch can help—either by being the owner of a stud dog or knowing one. Your vet could well know a suitable dog or you may have a friend who owns a male of the same breed.

Don't just choose any male dog of the right breed. Put the same amount of care and trouble into choosing the mate for your bitch as you did in choosing her as a puppy. Choose for temperament—a kind, placid dog. If yours is a breed in which there are any inherited disease control schemes—hip dysplasia or progressive retinal atrophy—try to find a dog that has been examined and obtained a certificate of freedom from these troubles.

Your actions in deciding to mate your bitch will result in any number up to 12 puppies being born, and becoming someone's pet of the future. It is quite irresponsible to breed without thinking of the 'good pet' qualities of the resulting litter.

We seem to have come a long way without getting to the point—an Englishman does need time—but the first crucial part of successful breeding is coming.

Mating. When? is the most important question. A bitch is on heat for 3 weeks but usually mating will not take place until at least the tenth day of heat—and in some cases much later. A good practical way is to try her with the dog on the eleventh day and then every 2 days until she will stand for the dog to mate. If the owner of the dog will allow it, let them mate on 2 occasions at the 2-day interval. The most fertile mating is as late in heat as the bitch will mate.

Allow a natural mating. Some—hopefully fewer each year—breeders will insist on holding a bitch who will not stand for the dog to mate. If the bitch is not prepared to mate it's our fault—we humans—for choosing the wrong time, and a 'forced' mating—a form of canine rape—is quite wrong.

My place or yours? If you can arrange it, bring the dog to the bitch. She'll be much more receptive in her own home, and a confusing, maybe tiring journey with missed meals is not conducive to good fertility. If you have to take the bitch for mating see if you can arrange to leave her for a few days and to arrive a day or so before mating time.

All the above is a counsel of perfection. Many litters result from single matings where the bitch is taken to the dog and returns home within an hour or so. But this illustrates the fertility of the bitch rather than the skill of human decision.

Mating itself may take any time between 5 and 45

minutes. The dog and bitch 'tie'—a perfectly normal happening. Any attempt to separate them during a tie can lead to injury of either. This applies if your bitch should go astray when on heat. If you find her at this crucial moment, wait until all is over. Buckets of water are not indicated. Let mating finish naturally. It is possible to give an injection within 24 hours of mating to prevent conception. This can be used to prevent 'accidental' puppies, but it is *not* a substitute for care. If you do not want your bitch to have puppies, keep her in, and do not let her mate.

Mating accomplished, you've got a wait of 63 days before puppies appear. The 63 days is not a magic figure, somewhere between 57 and 65 days is usual. A large litter tends to be a little earlier, one or two puppies only and a day or so over the 63 is usual. Don't forget to make a note of the mating date or dates. It can make life difficult for your veterinary surgeon if all that you can remember about the mating date is that it was a Thursday, two or three weeks after Good Friday—or was it Palm Sunday?

Unless one of your ancestors was the biblical Job, you'll be impatient to know if the mating was successful. The earliest that pregnancy can be detected is 21 days after mating. At this stage the individual puppies are not yet pea size but the afterbirth and puppies are round hard objects in the uterus about 1 inch in diameter. If your bitch is fairly slim and if she relaxes well, your veterinary surgeon may be able to palpate these enlargements in the abdomen. If this stage is missed, or not possible, the next fairly certain stage is about 45 days when the puppies themselves are solid enough to feel. In the occasional bitch with only a single puppy it is difficult to be certain until later still, but time will always tell. X-ray diagnosis of pregnancy is possible from about the 45th day—rarely necessary—and X-ray often means an anaesthetic to

keep the bitch still for a good picture, not a helpful
interference during pregnancy.

Enlargement of the udder and production of milk
is not a good guide to positive pregnancy. Because
false pregnancy is a normal happening after heat, milk
may be produced even after an infertile mating.

During pregnancy treat your bitch fairly normally.
You might find that she will need a little more food
in the last 3 weeks, but don't feed her for 6 from the
day of mating. Keep exercise going until the last 2 or 3
weeks, and if she wants to continue with plenty of
walks up to the day of whelping—she knows best.
A slightly lean bitch in 'hard' condition will whelp
much better than a flabby, obese, 'waddling' one.

Whelping is a normal happening—it's not a disease.
Remember this. Where should she be bedded down?
is the first question. The main requirements of the
whelping place are:

1. private
2. warm and dry
3. big enough for the bitch to stretch out in,
   and to accommodate the puppies for 2–3
   weeks.

Private may mean an unused bedroom, a shed outside, even a corner in the kitchen which can be shut
off by a screen—or even by a clothes-horse covered
in blankets. For the bitch that's very much part of the
household a 'kitchen corner' whelping allows her to
feel at home without being disturbed by every passing human.

Warm—means just that—not cooking. Somewhere around 70°F is a nice comfortable temperature.
Dryness is best obtained by some absorbent material
for the whelping box. Newspaper takes a lot of beat-
ing. It's cheap, free of any germs likely to matter to

the bitch, absorbent, easy to dispose of, and puppies cannot get tangled in it. Sometimes puppies get killed by the bitch lying on them, and rude things are said about clumsy bitches. In many cases it is possible that the owner/breeder was as much to blame by reason of providing blankets in which puppy got entangled and couldn't move out of mother's way.

The whelping box itself should be big enough— simply a matter of allowing six inches all round the bitch lying on her side. A front 2–4 inches high makes it easy for a heavily pregnant bitch to get over, tall enough to stop new-born puppies getting out. Let the other three sides be high enough to give privacy.

A whelping box need not be an expensive piece of furniture. A cardboard grocery box with one side cut out is adequate for smaller breeds. A similar construction in wood, made impervious by vinyl or polythene is within the competence of any local handyman or D.I.Y. enthusiast.

The Great Day. Whelping itself is a normal act, but if you're about to be granny to your bitch for the first time it's worth knowing what to expect and when to worry. Take your bitch to the vet a week or so beforehand. Apart from examining the mother-to-be, it's worth discussing normal whelping and it's also wise to find out how to contact your vet in the unlikely event of trouble during whelping. Normal whelping takes place over a period of many hours— there's no great emergency of 999 calls or rushing about connected with it. The first signs that things are about to happen are in the bitch's behaviour. She starts to make a bed, to appear uneasy and very often begins panting. This stage—true first stage labour— goes on for up to twelve hours and sometimes longer. She may take food and drink in this period, she may not. Offer food at normal feeding times and leave it to her to decide. Second stage labour—the actual birth of puppies—follows. She starts to strain to expel the puppy and within an hour of proper straining the first puppy should be born. Afterbirth may follow, either still attached to puppy or soon afterwards. Thereafter puppies will appear at intervals varying between a few minutes and 2 or 3 hours.

There are no magic times whereby you can decide that whelping is not normal, but a rough guide is that if 2 or 3 hours' straining does not produce a puppy something might be wrong, and if straining is very weak for 6 hours it's probably time to worry also.

If whelping takes place through the night there's no need to stay with her. Look at her very late, say midnight, get up and look at her in about 3 hours and if everything is all right *go back to bed*. Get up a bit earlier to see her again. No harm is going to come to her in the intervals, and an undisturbed bitch is better than one that you're worrying all through the night.

If you feel that she's in trouble, phone your vet, and be prepared to listen to his advice. He may say that everything seems normal and to wait a few hours—this doesn't mean he's uninterested—it means that he feels that your bitch doesn't want a stranger interfering. He may suggest that you bring the bitch to surgery—and if the whelping is a seriously abnormal one, surgery is the right place. Caesarean-delivery is a relatively safe method of dealing with serious whelping troubles—and your vet's surgery is a better place than your kitchen in which to do this operation. No bitch is likely to suffer any harm by this car journey.

In a normal whelping the bitch will deal with after-birth, cords, everything. She may eat the afterbirth—quite natural. Nature's way of hiding the fact that vulnerable young puppies are about.

One difficulty experienced by many owners is to know when the last puppy has arrived. If she's had 6, is there a seventh? Mum's behaviour will often tell you. Once all puppies have been born she'll settle down to nurse and feed them. Prior to that her attention is obviously divided between those that have been born and those still on the way. If you're not certain, get your vet to check her.

Apart from feeding mum, changing the paper bedding, there's little to do for the new family for the first 3 weeks. If the puppies' dewclaws are to be removed, this should be done (phone your vet again) around the third day. The eyes open at about 10 days and at about 3 weeks puppies begin to become active and want to leave their box and wander a little. If there's a big litter—six or more puppies—the strain of feeding them can begin to tell when they are about 3 weeks old. Almost any bitch can feed 6 or even 10 two-day-old puppies but by the time they are 3 weeks there's an awful lot more puppy to feed.

You can help mother by giving a little milk and chopped meat to the puppies from 3 weeks onwards. They begin to take more and more meat, less and less from mum. This also means that weaning is not a traumatic crisis—they slowly change from all mother's feed to hardly any, then none, and the strain on mother is reduced.

Years ago every mother-to-be was reduced to a state of terror by graphic descriptions of her Aunt Winnie's confinements. Newcomers to dog breeding can be similarly worried even today. Here are a few things that happen and can be quite normal.

A deep green discharge is normal as part of the afterbirth. When you see this on white newspaper it looks terrible but it is quite normal if you see it *after* a puppy has been born. If you see such a discharge before the first puppy is born it could mean that there is some abnormal delay in birth.

The bitch often carries puppies in her mouth, and a nervous bitch will pick them up too roughly if she's excited. Gentle handling, as little disturbance as possible and, if she'll take it, a big meal can help. A full tummy is a good sedative.

The same rather nervous bitch might pant heavily when she's feeding her puppies or even when she sees you. Again, it's a nervous reaction—or a full bladder. The proud new mother sometimes will not leave her precious puppies even for a minute and she sits there with a nearly bursting bladder getting more and more uncomfortable—and panting. If you take her out she'll urinate very soon, and profusely. Once relieved she'll return to the puppies feeling comfortable.

No doubt there are many other matters connected with breeding dogs that are not mentioned here. If there is anything missing that worries you—phone your vet or take your bitch to see him. That's why he's there.

Old age

'Till death us do part' was the first phrase in this book. The average life span of a dog is about one sixth of the average life of his owner. So three or four times in your lifetime you'll meet old age—true senile decay—in your pet.

Old age

One might define old age as that period of life when the various bits and pieces that make up the living body begin to wear out.

The commonest organs to wear out are the kidneys, the filters of the body, and their wear means that waste products are not removed, so the dog becomes poisoned by his own waste products. When the kidneys are beginning to fail, Nature tries to help by giving the dog an excessive thirst. The more he drinks, the more urine he passes and this 'flushing' action means that for a time more waste is removed and ill health does not result. This does not work for every dog. Sooner or later the extra water is not enough and uraemia—the build-up of waste products in the blood—occurs and so does very serious illness. This is not a veterinary textbook but this explanation might help you to understand why an excessive thirst might be a sign of serious trouble. The early kidney troubles can often be treated very satisfactorily, but the 'wear out' situation in the older dog is always serious sooner or later.

Other organs might degenerate first, the liver or the heart, for example. Some malignant tumours occur in old age.

Inevitably something goes wrong to constitute an incurable situation which is synonymous with 'old age'. These problems occur only in protected animals—pet animals and human beings. Farm animals are usually slaughtered when their economic life is finished, wild animals succumb to predators, to starvation or are killed in fights when they become too old, too slow to find or catch food, to run or to fight. Nature has a system of euthanasia, crude though it may be.

It sounds very nice to say 'Let him die naturally'—in fact this is usually not nice, for dog or owner, and you have to make a decision: should you have your dog treated or should he be destroyed?

It's never easy. When your dog has been part of the family for fourteen years or so it is difficult to make decisions on a logical basis, but if you can detach yourself from emotion it is likely that your decision will be a correct one and in the interests of your pet. Your veterinary surgeon can and will help you. He'll certainly tell you if, in his opinion, it is unreasonable to keep the dog alive. But often there's a grey area.

The dog is not suffering actual pain, on the other hand he's getting little pleasure from life. This is where you can help, can help your dog, if you can detach yourself and try to decide—with your vet—if it's fair to keep the dog. Try to 'add up' a week. If he has a miserable morning one day, but he's bright and cheerful for the rest of the week, all right, but if most days are miserable, spent in a vague limbo and only a few hours of apparent enjoyment, why prolong his life?

Remember your dog does not know what is wrong. If there is a malignant tumour, if there is an incurable situation, your dog does not know. What he feels matters, not what might be wrong. If there is any pain, try to consider if this is reasonable. An old dog often has aches and pains, rheumaticky 'twinges', so do we. A few minutes' ache, or even real pain when he gets up in the morning is not a reason for putting him to sleep if the rest of the twenty-four hours are pain-free and enjoyable. In any case it's probable that the pain can be well controlled by treatment. But if there's pain that might be prolonged, if the very old dog is badly injured in a road accident, it might be unreasonable to ask him to suffer this because the time left to him is so short. One might accept it as fair that a two-year-old dog has a very uncomfortable, even painful fortnight after a road accident if he's going to have ten or more normal years afterwards, but the old dog in the last few months of life cannot be offered a fair exchange for his fortnight's pain.

If you can think in this way you'll be fair to your dog. Everyone is fallible and no one can decide the exact moment when it becomes unreasonable to prolong life, but you can try and can feel that you have made the right decision in the interest of your dog.

If euthanasia has to be this is best done at the surgery. The usual method is by injection of a massive overdose of anaesthetic into a vein. Injecting into a vein is a slightly specialized procedure and it is essential to have good light and a properly held dog. One of the surgery staff—used to handling animals—can assist much better than you. It's not her dog and it is her job, so a calm and efficient injection can ensue; these injections are never painful but a nervous owner can transmit fear to the dog. With a nervous dog it is possible to give a tranquillizer first so that there is no panic, no fear.

Again, ask your vet—maybe it's something that you can discuss years before the time comes. After death comes the problem of what to do with the body. This depends on your wishes and circumstances. Burial in the garden, disposal by the Local Council or cremation are available.

The law

Once upon a time there were two certainties—death and taxes. Now, as a result of the indefatigable efforts of our legislators there are three—and the third is the law. Whatever you do—well, nearly everything—concerns the law and the dog and his owner are no exceptions.

Many Acts apply to the dog owner, and in writing about them let us start by saying that this is not a legal treatise, it is probably correct at the time of going to press, that this is a veterinary surgeon's account of the law and not a lawyer's and finally, to borrow a phrase from the legal profession, all that follows is 'without prejudice'.

Dogs Acts abound. The first was 1871, then 1906, amendments in 1928 and 1938. You still need a licence to keep a dog more than six months old, although this may change in the future. The cost is 37p, a halfpenny less than in 1871, and it is obtained from a Post Office.

If your dog causes trouble to neighbours by biting them or their dogs, a court may make an order for the dog to be kept under control, or may order it to be destroyed. It is not true that every dog is allowed one bite.

A stray dog must be taken by the finder to the nearest Police Station, the Police then have an obligation to keep the dog and provide all necessary food and attention for 7 days. If your dog strays and you claim him later, the Police may recover from you all the expenses incurred on behalf of your dog.

The Control of Dogs Order 1930 requires every dog on the highway or in a public place to wear a collar bearing its owner's name and address. Working dogs and hounds are exempt.

The Control of Dogs Order, 1930

Many towns and cities make by-laws or use regulations under the Control of Dogs Order to require that all dogs are kept under control from sunset to sunrise and kept on a lead at all times when on the roads.

Further by-laws may regulate the toilet activities of your dog. Many districts make it an offence to allow dogs to foul the pavement. Penalties may be up to £20—an expensive spending of a penny.

The Animals Act 1971 makes you responsible for damage caused by your animal—dog, horse, cow or what have you. So if your Great Dane is in collision with a motor car you could be liable in law for damage caused to the car and injury to the driver. You are also liable if your dog injures or kills sheep or poultry, and under certain circumstances a farmer may shoot a dog on his land if he believes that the dog may worry his cattle, sheep or any livestock.

Importation of dogs is strictly controlled, and except for dogs from Eire, any dog imported into the U.K. must spend 6 months in quarantine at an approved kennel. Landings are only allowed at certain specified ports and airports and an import licence must be obtained before any dog (or other animal) is imported.

Penalties for infringement may be high: £1,000 fine plus imprisonment and possible destruction of the dog.

Such measures may appear draconian, but they are essential to prevent the introduction of rabies into this country, and almost any steps are justified to maintain our present freedom from this killer disease.

Regardless of your attitude to 'law and order', observance of the letter and spirit of all the regulations

To smuggle a dog into this country is not the act of a devoted dog lover

concerned with rabies prevention is the public duty
of all. You may be tempted to bring an extra bottle
or a new watch through Customs—and we could be
persuaded to wish you well. But any attempt to defeat
the vigilance of Customs Officers and to smuggle a
dog into this country is not the act of a devoted dog
lover, it's the action of a supremely selfish maniac.

Let's retire from the pulpit and back to the law,
which is concerned with protecting your dog.

Cruelty in general terms is covered by the 1911
Protection of Animals Act. Amongst other things this
Act makes it an offence to cause unnecessary suffering
by any means. It is an offence to use a dog for drawing
carts or trucks, and a Police Constable may authorize
a veterinary surgeon to destroy any animal to relieve
unreasonable suffering.

Transport of all animals, and thus dogs, is governed
by the Transit of Animals (General) Order 1973,
which regulates shipment by rail, road, air or sea. It
regulates the size of crate, the intervals between feeding and watering. It even regulates the transport of
tortoises which is a very good thing.

It is an offence to use a dog for drawing carts

If you buy your dog from a pet shop, the shop must be licensed under the Pet Animals Act 1951, and if you ever see or visit a pet shop and there are animals in conditions you feel are undesirable, the local council is the responsible body who grant the licence.

Similarly, if you board your dog the kennels will be licensed by the local council—the Animal Boarding Establishments Act 1963.

Since 1974, dog breeders have been subject to regulation by the Breeding of Dogs Act 1973 which came into effect on 1 April 1974. Every person owning more than two bitches for the business of breeding dogs must be licensed.

That's not all but it's probably all that really matters and in any event the law does not concern or concern itself with the reasonable, responsible dog owner. Just as in 'Z Cars', it's the villains that matter be they human or canine.

How to treat your vet

We're not talking about whether he takes sugar in his coffee or water in whisky but how to treat your veterinary surgeon so that you, and your dog, get the greatest possible value and greatest possible advantage from the vet's time and knowledge, and the fee you pay him.

Modern (nationalized) medicine has probably brainwashed you into an acceptance of the fact that medical and veterinary time is precious. So it is, but a veterinary surgeon exists to be consulted—he'd starve otherwise. The first thing to believe is that if you are concerned about your dog's well-being it is right and proper to take him to your vet. Should it turn out that all your worries were groundless, that the funny lump, funny behaviour are normal things that happen, don't, please, go away feeling foolish. A vet's job is as much to advise the owner as treat the dog.

If you are ever worried, see your vet, and not in the half-apologetic way of 'I'm sorry to waste your time, but ...'

On the other hand, try to be clear in your own mind what has happened to the dog, when it happened and in what way you are concerned.

We cannot ask the dog. You must speak on his behalf and if your information is garbled, inaccurate or incomplete the diagnosis is that much less accurate, the advice is less good and the dog less happy. These are the sorts of things that happen, and not all apocryphal stories. Undue modesty causes trouble—most families have their own private terms for various bodily functions—but when one is presented with a dog and told 'His number one's all right but when he did his duty this morning number two was a bit funny', there is a tendency to look for an electronic calculator to solve this mathematical problem. 'She's not very well' can be a confusing euphemism for a bitch on heat.

Young children sent to a veterinary surgeon accompanied only by their pet can lead to considerable difficulties and complications. First, children cannot, in law, authorize treatment, anaesthesia, or destruction. It is not always certain that children will remember advice or instructions about treatment, but this selective memory also occurs in adults.

If you have to let your children take the dog to your vet, send a clearly written note and, if possible, include a telephone number so that you can be contacted. A ten- or twelve-year-old may know very little about his 'own' pet.

All veterinary surgeons are quite happy to see a dog with children (well controlled) present alongside parents, but not children unaccompanied, please. You're not very popular if this goes too far. On one occasion 12 children plus rabbit and mother (children's) appeared in the waiting room. It was someone's birthday and the highlight of the afternoon was a visit to the vet's. Sound economics—cinema seats for 12 are expensive but that much party spirit in a waiting room was disastrous.

So, Rule One. Think about your dog before you visit the vet, think about what you want to say, use as precise words as you can. Faeces, urine, diarrhoea, anus, penis, vagina are all acceptable and, more important still, exact words. 'Number one', 'number two', 'runny', 'back there' and 'you know' are very confusing.

Rule Two. Decide what you want. In some instances of serious troubles you have to decide whether you want your dog treated or to have him destroyed. This is your decision. Your vet can, will and should advise, but you must decide. If you really don't want treatment, say so. Vets are skilful but mind reading is not one of their attributes.

Rule Three. Ask questions, no matter how silly you might fear they are. If something is worrying you this is a totally adequate reason for consulting your vet. You are not wasting his time. If there is trouble you'll have to find out and sooner may allow treatment, while later will not.

If there is a funny lump developing somewhere on your dog and you are worried that it might be cancer, *ask*. Sometimes we see the lump, which could be an abscess, a cyst, a totally non-malignant harmless growth, yet because the owner does not ask 'Is it cancer?' the reassurance that could have been so certainly given is left unsaid. The owner didn't like to ask, the vet never knew the question was there.

Lots of the other rules you've heard before in a medical context. Phone early in the day—before 10 a.m. Home visits are inevitably more expensive, and sometimes less efficient than coming to the surgery. At the surgery there is help to hold the dog, all facilities, all drugs which cannot be available at a house call. There's usually better reception on the part of the owner—no radio playing, no baker calling, no childish crisis occurring upstairs or in the garden.

Night and other out-of-hours emergencies happen. With a little advance preparation these crises can be less disastrous. Find out from your vet how he arranges for emergency calls. Is there a special night telephone number? Is there a telephone answering machine giving an alternative night number? Ask in the cold light of day and you won't be confused on a dark night.

Finally, a plea to women or, in particular, some wives. Cultivate the art of decision. So many late emergency calls result from the wife not being willing to phone until her husband has come home and had his tea. So the dog who broke his leg at 10 a.m. has to wait until 8 p.m. before someone phones for attention. What would happen if the house were on fire? A nuisance for the vet who was looking forward to going home, an unnecessarily miserable day for the dog who could have been seen to and made less uncomfortable much earlier. And it will probably cost more.

Index